BRITAIN INTO EUROPE

Britain Into Europe

PUBLIC OPINION AND THE EEC 1961-75

Edited by
ROGER JOWELL and GERALD HOINVILLE

CROOM HELM LONDON

First Published 1976
© 1976 By Social & Community Planning Research

Croom Helm Ltd, 2–10 St. John's Road, London, SW11

ISBN 0 85664 264 9

Printed in Great Britain by Biddles Ltd, Guildford, Surrey

CONTENTS

Foreword   1

Acknowledgements   2

Notes on Contributors   3

1 An Unconscionable Time Deciding
   Roger Jowell and Gerald Hoinville   5

2 Movements in the Public Mood: 1961-75
   James Spence   18

3 The Final Four Years: From Opposition to Endorsement
   Barry Hedges   37

4 The Media and the Messages
   Dipak Nandy   77

5 Who Voted What
   Martin Collins   92

6 The Changing Constitution
   Andrew Duff   109

Index   124

FOREWORD

This book stems from the unique event of 5 June 1975 when the British people settled a long-standing controversy over their country's membership of the European Economic Community. The chapters are based largely on the work of researchers within Social and Community Planning Research (SCPR), an independent institute for social survey research with which all but one of the contributors are connected.

The long debate about Britain's relationship with her European neighbours was characterised by an atmosphere of uncertainty and schizophrenia that the referendum has momentarily — at least — dispersed. The extended and often bitter argument has now been relegated to the status of a minor quarrel. Our aim here is to document and to diagnose the movement in public attitudes towards the EEC, from apathy, through antipathy, to support, adducing our evidence primarily from three SCPR studies carried out between 1971 and 1975, and from opinion polls undertaken by other organisations over a longer period. A subsidiary theme is the issue of Britain's first national referendum, an issue that became almost inseparable from the question it was designed to resolve.

Although we have included a chapter on the political background to Britain's postwar relationship with Western Europe, we have resisted including one on the well-documented standpoints of the pro- and anti-market lobbies over the same period. They are covered here only in so far as their 'official' lines are mirrored in the public's perception of the issues. We have tried, however, to capture the mood of the debate, the events and the personalities that combined to produce this piece of contemporary history.

ACKNOWLEDGEMENTS

This volume owes its existence to the financial support given by three organisations for the surveys on which Chapter 3 is based: the *European Educational Research Trust*, who grant-aided SCPR's 1971 and 1974 studies, the *Commission of the European Communities*, who sponsored the fieldwork of the 1975 study, and the *Social Science Research Council*, who funded the combined analysis of the 1974 and 1975 data. We are very grateful to all of them.

We are also indebted to Isobel Campbell of SCPR for her editorial advice and assistance on the many drafts of the manuscripts that finally turned into the chapters of this book; to six secretaries within SCPR — Sheila Brennan, Vikki Gladwell, Pat O'Donnell, Christine Russo, Hemali Seneviratne and Gillian Sibley — for their good humour, patience and skill in the typing and re-typing of the manuscripts; to our colleagues in Centre for Sample Surveys, particularly Colin Airey, Sandra Chuter, Jenny Harvey, Trevor James, Daphne Steggals, David and Norma Walker, for their valuable work in organising the surveys described in Chapter 3; to the anonymous interviewers who gathered the raw material from all over the country on which the interpretations are based; and to the many authors, cited in the chapter references, from whom we have gleaned so much background information.

NOTES ON CONTRIBUTORS

Martin Collins is a research director of SCPR. An economics graduate, he has worked in survey research since 1962. He has lectured and published on a range of research topics, has contributed to two basic textbooks on the subject, and is co-author – with G. J. Goodhardt and A. S. C. Ehrenberg – of the book *The Television Audience: Patterns of Viewing* (Saxon House, 1975).

Andrew Duff read history at St John's College, Cambridge, and has since studied the politics of the European Communities both at Cambridge and at the Institut d'Etudes Européennes in Brussels. Currently he is Research Officer to the Hansard Society's programme on the effects of EEC membership on Britain's representative institutions.

Barry Hedges graduated from Cambridge in 1955 and since then has been continuously engaged in sample survey research. His first project as research director at SCPR, which he joined in 1971, was the survey of attitudes to the EEC, and he has subsequently directed a number of major research projects dealing with various aspects of public attitudes and preferences.

Gerald Hoinville graduated in economics and statistics in 1960 and then joined a market research agency. Later, as a director of that company, he created a planning/transport research group and headed the company's statistics unit. In 1969 he left to become co-founder and co-director of SCPR where he has continued to develop survey methods and statistical techniques for use in a wide range of transport, planning and social problems.

Roger Jowell is an economics graduate who has specialised in social survey research for the past eleven years. As co-founder and co-director of SCPR, he has been responsible for a broad range of attitudinal and behavioural studies, among them the 1971 survey of attitudes to the EEC (with Barry Hedges), the 1974 survey (with James Spence) and the 1975 survey (with Barry Hedges and James Spence). He has written and lectured widely on social research methods.

3

Dipak Nandy formerly lecturer in English at the University of Leicester; lecturer at the University of Kent at Canterbury; first director of the Runnymede Trust 1968-73; subsequently joined SCPR. Although a member of the Committee on the Future of Broadcasting (Chairman Lord Annan), he contributes to this volume in his personal capacity.

James Spence took his Masters degree in political behaviour and has worked in survey research since 1968, joining SCPR in 1973. He is co-author (with Frank Teer) of the book *Political Opinion Polls* (Hutchinsons University Libraries). He has lectured on statistics and social research and published articles on these topics. He has conducted several social surveys, particularly on political attitudes, including the 1974 and 1975 SCPR surveys on attitudes towards the EEC (with Roger Jowell and Barry Hedges).

1 AN UNCONSCIONABLE TIME DECIDING

Roger Jowell and Gerald Hoinville

The verdict has been given by a vote and a majority bigger than that achieved by any government in a general election in the history of our democracy . . . It means that fourteen years of national argument are over. — Harold Wilson, outside 10 Downing Street on 6 June 1975, as the final referendum results were coming in.

The sense of relief in Harold Wilson's words echoed a national sense of relief. It extended even to ardent opponents of the referendum and to many passionate anti-Europeans. The result and the method of achieving it were now less important than the fact that the long and often dull debate had been resolutely concluded.

Britain could have been in at the beginning, when the idea of a European Community was first being canvassed in the immediate postwar years. But the government was reluctant on several counts: Britain was more influential and stronger economically than the other potential members; she had emerged undefeated from the Second World War; she never believed that France and Germany could forge close ties; she led the Commonwealth; she saw herself as an international power responsible for ordering world affairs and equivalent in status to the USA and the Soviet Union. Although those grandiose self-images were soon to fade and were crumbling fast by the time that the EEC was inaugurated in 1957, Britain had already talked herself out of membership.

It was not long before the British government recognised its misjudgement: Britain applied to join the club in 1961. Indeed, had it not been for the intransigence of President de Gaulle, the application might well have succeeded. In the event, two more attempts and twelve years passed before Britain was finally accepted. And another two years went by before the British public had endorsed the government's decision to sign the Treaty of Accession.

It is intriguing to speculate how the public would have reacted if we had entered the EEC at the first attempt. Would the Labour Party and the trade unions willingly have participated in the activities and institutions of the European Communities? Would the public have

5

embraced membership more enthusiastically in 1961 than it was to do in 1973? There is no doubt that in 1973, when it seemed that the matter had been resolved, the public greeted the fact of EEC membership with overwhelming diffidence. Yet in 1975, when the British people were given their first chance in history to assume the role of legislators, their verdict seemed assured and convincing. We were, at last, Europeans. Or were we? The survey data described by Barry Hedges in Chapter 3 argue persuasively that, for many people, the decision was a last-minute one: we were only just Europeans; full-hearted numerical consent concealed a very faint-hearted emotional consent. Despite the size of the majority, it was, in Wellington's words, 'a damn'd close-run thing'.

Before examining the changes in public opinion on the EEC over the last fifteen years, we look back in this chapter at the changes in the postures of successive governments towards the EEC over that period. Their *voltes faces* have been no less numerous than the public's, and, arguably, no less inexplicable.

Just good friends

Three main factors promoted the demands for European unity in the late 1940s. First, the postwar years, like all postwar years, were characterised by strong pressures for international cooperation and unity: the UN was formed in 1945, as was the International Monetary Fund, in an atmosphere of renewed hope and high ideals. Second, and in contrast, the war had brought in its wake a pervasive fear of future wars between different adversaries: the Atlantic Alliance was formed in 1949. Third, within Europe, there was a determination to control Western Germany, not by domination or discrimination, but by economic and political cooperation: the Western European Union was formed in 1948, the Organisation for European Economic Cooperation and the Council of Europe in 1949.

Although Britain played an active part in all the European initiatives, she clearly saw her own role elsewhere, in a much wider context. Yes, Britain was in Europe but not *only* in Europe. She was a major world power who owed her allegiances and attentions to world groupings. She saw the need for western European unity and would sponsor and encourage it. But to think of Britain as just a western European nation would have been to belittle her national and international status. Britain was, after all, equally interested in preserving the unity of the Commonwealth (under her leadership). And she took her role as one of the leaders of the newly formed NATO seriously. In the heady postwar

years, Britain would have considered a stridently European posture far
too parochial. Europe began at Calais; if Britain had a consistent stance
at all, it was as a warm but detached supporter: 'France and Germany
must take the lead together. Great Britain . . . America and I trust
Soviet Russia . . . must be friends and sponsors of the new Europe'
(Winston Churchill, 1946). At moments, however, Britain moved closer
to Europe. In a now famous speech in the House of Commons in 1948,
Ernest Bevin, foreign secretary in the postwar years, tacitly placed
Britain firmly in the context of a new Europe:

> '. . . the free nations of Western Europe must now draw closely
> together. These nations have a great deal in common — their war-
> time sacrifices, their hatred of injustice and oppression, their
> parliamentary democracy, their efforts to promote economic justice,
> their understanding and love of liberty. I believe the time is ripe for
> a consolidation of Western Europe . . . We are thinking now of
> Western Europe as a unit.'

The speech excited the immediate interest of European federalists
such as Paul-Henri Spaak of Belgium, who later described Bevin as *the*
foreign minister who gave the European Movement its initial impulse',
and as 'a great European'. But the excitement did not last; Bevin
later tried to minimise the significance of what he had said and, in the
end, his speech did not herald the new era it had promised. Britain
returned to her detached posture and the moment had gone — the
'one moment in her political history', according to Spaak, when 'Britain
was enthusiastic and, may I say, lucid, about Europe'.
    Her renewed detachment led Britain to reject membership of the
European Coal and Steel Community — the forerunner of the EEC. As
always, Britain was keen to maintain liaison, eager to cooperate, but
adamantly unwilling to relinquish sovereignty. Her attitude was summed
up vividly by Harold Macmillan, then in opposition, in 1950: 'Our
people will not hand over to a supranational authority the right to
close down our pits and our steelworks.' The Coal and Steel Community was created, without Britain, in 1951. By 1955, its members ('the
Six') had given up trying to woo Britain. They did not invite Britain to
their formal conference called to set up the EEC. They were resigned to
Britain's rejection of integration and determined to prove that integration could work. Britain's response was predictable: she would cooperate with the Six, but she would not become a seventh. Instead she
proposed a free trade area between the Six and the original OEEC

countries. Britain wanted to avoid the trade penalties of being an out-
sider. But she also wanted to avoid the constraints of membership. Not
surprisingly, her proposal was rejected and the Treaty of Rome was
signed in 1957.

The start of something serious

The late 1950s and early 1960s witnessed a strengthening of European
economies in comparison with Britain's. The formation of the EEC
may have been one explanation for this trend, but there were others.
First, the Commonwealth was a declining market for British exports;
second, the European Free Trade Area (EFTA), of which Britain was a
member, had never worked as well as the EEC; third, Britain's
productivity had been growing much more slowly than that of her
neighbours. Moreover, as the Six had all been either defeated or occupied during the war, their postwar economic reconstruction was generally more fundamental than Britain's. It was beginning to show results.

Politically, also, Britain was moving into a new era. The Suez affair
in 1956 had already eroded British self-confidence and created strains
within the Commonwealth and the Atlantic Alliance; Britain's colonies
were quickly becoming independent nations with independent voices;
the cold war was at its iciest, thus confirming the United States and the
Soviet Union as the undisputed leaders of the two world blocs. Britain's
recognition that she was no longer an independent military power
became explicit when she abandoned the Blue Streak missile in 1960,
the same year as the collapse of the Paris summit conference. By that
time, also, the 'special relationship' between the USA and Britain was
no longer very special.

Despite Britain's weakening economic and political position, the
general election of 1959 could still be fought on the 'never had it so
good' theme. It was to be the last British election for *at least* two
decades that could conceivably have involved that slogan. (Contrast it,
for example, with the Conservative's 1964 election theme of 'better the
devil you know'!)

With the aid of the exact science of hindsight, therefore, we can see
how inevitable it was that before very long Britain would look to the
successful European Community. And, in 1961, Edward Heath, as Lord
Privy Seal in the Macmillan government, was appointed leader of
Britain's negotiating team to take Britain into the EEC. The fourteen
years of national argument had begun:

'. . . as a result of a thorough assessment over a considerable period

of the needs of our own country, of Europe and of the Free World
as a whole ... we desire to become full, wholehearted and active
members of the European Community in its widest sense and to go
forward with you in the building of a new Europe' (Edward Heath,
1961).

But there was a snag in the shape of President de Gaulle, a comparative
newcomer to peacetime European politics. He had never liked the
Treaty of Rome but was now to use it adroitly to strengthen the
French position in the EEC out of all proportion to her political,
economic or military status. He was always suspicious of Britain's
motives for seeking to join the EEC and, in any case, he felt that
British membership would weaken the French position. He was to use
his veto in January 1963 to prevent, for the time being, any change in
the European *status quo*.

The timing of the veto was significant. Although it had been pres-
aged for some months, it eventually came swiftly after a Bermuda
meeting between Harold Macmillan and John Kennedy at which
Britain agreed to buy Polaris nuclear missiles. The deal confirmed all
de Gaulle's (and others') suspicions: Britain was not European; she
was an American satellite. To allow Britain into Europe would be to
open the door to Anglo-American dominance, the antithesis of the
European dream.

In the next chapter, James Spence describes the state of British
public opinion during this phase of our EEC negotiations. Here we need
only comment on the pattern of political opinion at the time, a pattern
that was to prove remarkably robust in essence if not in detail. There
was some suspicion of the EEC in all parties. Whereas the Conservatives
and Liberals were officially in favour of British membership, however,
the Labour Party under Hugh Gaitskell was officially circumspect. It
was not against membership on any terms, but the terms it wanted
were unlikely to be attainable.

The opposition on grounds of principle came mainly from the left
of the Labour Party and from the right of the Conservative Party. The
former regarded the EEC as a 'bonanza for capitalism' or, in Wilson's
words of 1961, 'a highly restrictive, highly discriminating trading
bloc'. The right had its more chauvinistic objections to the EEC; Lord
Selbourne, for example, felt that British membership of the EEC
would 'be at the expense of sacrificing our imperial heritage ... The
continental nations may be charming neighbours and good friends, but
they are not to be preferred to our own kith and kin who owe

allegiance to the Queen'. Fears for the future of the Commonwealth – on grounds other than those expressed by Lord Selbourne – were frequently raised. Members of all parties were concerned that membership of the EEC would mark an end to Britain's traditional duty to the developing countries of Asia, Africa and the Caribbean; others placed more emphasis on British links with Australia, New Zealand and Canada. In the event, the veto ended the argument. Nothing was to change for the moment.

A long courtship

Hugh Gaitskell's death in 1963 brought Harold Wilson to the leadership of the Labour Party, and he was to become the dominant figure in British politics during the 1960s and 1970s. Under his leadership, Labour went on to win two general elections in quick succession – the 1964 election just, and the 1966 election comfortably. But the economic problems that had been exposed some ten years earlier had now become an endemic feature of our national life. In particular, the monthly balance of payments figures had been elevated from anonymity in the financial columns of the press to prominence in front page banner headlines. Harold Macmillan had given way as Conservative leader to Sir Alec Douglas Home, who, after the 1964 election defeat had given way in turn to Edward Heath. After the relative calm of the 1950s, these were times of continual political drama.

Harold Wilson had never been a 'European' in the way that Edward Heath or George Brown, then deputy Prime Minister, had always been. But he knew that something had to be done to improve Britain's trading position, and in November 1966 Britain's negotiations started with the EEC. By May 1967 a formal application for membership was on the table. All three political parties were now in favour of Britain's entry, though the Labour Party still contained more than its fair share of sceptics.

Looking back, it is not surprising that opposition to the EEC within the Labour Party was at its lowest at that time. Harold Wilson's personal popularity was not wholly responsible for this. Two other factors contributed. First, Britain's dependence on America for loans to tide her over the economic crises had created anger and resentment among the Labour left, especially during the Vietnam war. They thought that this dependence explained the Labour government's failure to condemn America's military involvement in South-east Asia. It must be remembered that the Vietnam war was at this time the *cause célebre* of Labour constituency parties. So although the EEC was a 'capitalist club', it was not, perhaps, as tainted as the Anglo-American club. Second, by this time de Gaulle had become identified as the scourge of American foreign policy. He wanted to build Europe up as an alternative world bloc; his relations with Eastern European countries and China were cordial; he was backing out of NATO. All these policies drew sympathy from British Labour Party activists. If this was to be the new Europe, it would not be so bad after all.

Once again, however, a moment of British enthusiasm for Europe was wasted. A second veto by de Gaulle in November 1967 — by which time British public opinion had turned against the EEC — removed the issue temporarily from the public gaze, but not from the political agenda. Britain was not going to give up.

de Gaulle's individual style was now creating strains within the EEC. He was asserting his independence from the Western bloc, as evidenced by his support for the Arab states in their conflict with Israel and his *'Vive le Québec libre'* speech. And he was blocking progress towards economic and monetary integration in Europe. West Germany was getting stronger economically and becoming restive at French attempts to dominate the EEC. Then came a series of events that caused de Gaulle to falter badly.

In May 1968, there were internal riots and strikes: the French President was no longer in control domestically; he was forced to introduce social reforms and wages policies that were drastically to change France's economic situation; a severe monetary crisis developed; in the end, he was forced to accept American support for a major French loan negotiated through the IMF. In August 1968, the Soviet Union's invasion of Czechoslovakia was a severe setback to de Gaulle's concept of a united Europe. In any case, West Germany's refusal to revalue her currency as a means of taking pressure off the French franc had already created hostility between France and Germany. If there was ever a time when de Gaulle was sympathetic to British entry into the EEC, it was now. He even flirted publicly with the idea of a new political Europe in which France and Britain could play dominant roles.

But de Gaulle was not to be the architect of a new Europe; in 1969, after the French people had rejected his advice in a referendum, he resigned the presidency and left the political stage he had occupied with such panache for nearly a decade.

Marriage at last

With the villain of the piece now safely out of the way, Harold Wilson could reopen negotiations on Britain's application, which had in any case been 'left on the table'. It seemed prudent, however, to let Georges Pompidou, the new French President, settle in before pressing ahead. Negotiations were scheduled to start in mid-1970, following a six-month period during which the EEC countries would establish a common negotiating position. Hopes were now high that Britain's persistence would at last be rewarded. But the *dénouement* had to wait: Harold Wilson chose June 1970 as the time for a British general election.

The manifestoes of the main parties all included commitments to British membership of the EEC, qualified only by *caveats* about the nature of the final terms:

> 'Only when we negotiate will it be possible to determine whether the balance is a fair one and in the interests of Britain' (Conservative manifesto).

> '. . . if satisfactory terms cannot be secured in the negotiations, Britain will be able to stand on her own feet outside the Community' (Labour manifesto).

The unanimity of the parties on the question of British entry was later to become a major political issue: the views of anti-European electors had been given no outlet in the form of a vote for any of the major parties.

To everyone's surprise, Mr Heath, the original European negotiator and advocate, won the election and was thus able to continue the process he had started nearly ten years before. And now he had, so he thought, the full support of the opposition Labour Party.

Negotiations started in an atmosphere that gave Heath and his negotiators little cause for concern: the EEC countries were all pressing France to admit Britain and the other applicants (at that stage, Denmark, Norway and Ireland: Norway was to withdraw after its own referendum on the issue in 1972). They felt that enlargement of the EEC would make it stronger economically and politically. And they were in a good position to put pressure on France since the twelve year 'period of transition' for the joint economic policies of the Six had just ended, and the French government was anxious about what the new agricultural policy of the EEC might be. The threat of a third French veto was therefore bargained away in exchange for concessions on agriculture. By that time, French public opinion was also moving in favour of admitting Britain: a survey published early in 1971 suggested that nearly two out of every three people in France thought British

membership of the EEC would be of mutual benefit to Britain and
Europe.

But stirrings at home put an end to any possible danger of euphoria
on the part of Mr Heath. Public opinion in Britain was moving further
against membership. By the summer of 1971 it was about 2:1 against
entry; among Labour Party supporters it was about 4:1 against. The
TUC was becoming increasingly antagonistic to the prospect of membership, as were Labour Party activists at all levels. Wilson was embarrassed,
since he had started on the path that Heath was now treading. But he
had the *caveat* from his manifesto to deploy: his party's attitude to
membership would depend on the terms; he could not and would not
commit his party in advance of the terms.

The White Paper containing the negotiated terms was published in
July 1971. Its reception in the Labour Party was mixed. George
Thomson, Labour's ex-negotiator, and Michael Stewart, Labour's ex-
foreign secretary, both said that the terms were identical to the ones
they had anticipated and would have accepted when in office. Labour's
Party Conference later rejected the terms and, finally, so did Wilson.
At a meeting of the Parliamentary Labour Party he proposed the
motion opposing entry on the Tory terms: the motion was carried by
159 votes to 89. A week later, on 28 October 1971, Wilson led his
party — with a three-line whip in the House of Commons — against the
Bill that committed Britain to enter the EEC on the negotiated terms.
Despite the whip, sixty-nine Labour MPs voted with the government
and twenty more abstained. The voting figures were 356 in favour of
membership, 244 against, an overall pro-EEC majority of 112. The
majority, though larger than had been anticipated, was depressed
slightly by a similar rebellion against the leadership by thirty-nine
Conservative MPs who voted against membership and two more who
abstained.

It was at about this time that the idea of a referendum began to gain
national currency, though it had been canvassed earlier, particularly
by Tony Benn. Three powerful arguments were being advanced in its
favour. First, Edward Heath had promised earlier that Britain would
not enter the EEC without the full-hearted consent of Parliament *and*
people; second, as we have observed, EEC membership had not been an
election issue; third, unprecedented constitutional issues were at
stake — issues that involved our independence and sovereignty as a
nation. Despite the growing clamour from the protagonists of a referendum, however, the government was clearly unwilling to go back on
the declared will of Parliament. In vote after vote in the House of

Commons it carried narrow parliamentary majorities for the remaining stages of the Act that would take us into Europe. (By now the Labour rebels were voting with their party against the government.)

The issue was resolved after twelve years: on 1 January 1973, the United Kingdom, Denmark and Eire were admitted to membership of the EEC. Denmark and Eire had held referenda and obtained majorities for going in. The United Kingdom had not; in her case, Parliament had decided on behalf of the people. It was not to remain so.

A question of annulment

Until the year or two preceding Britain's entry into the EEC, few people regarded a referendum as an appropriate device for taking the decision. As the prospect of membership became more likely, so the demands for a referendum grew more vociferous. Now that Britain was in the EEC, instead of dying down the movement continued to gather strength. Plainly, the opponents of British membership saw a referendum as the only conceivable method of getting Britain out of the EEC. They were not persuaded that membership was a *fait accompli*. In retrospect, the change was remarkable: only three years earlier, Britain's rejection of the referendum device had been the one apparent certainty in domestic politics:

'I don't think you can govern in this country by referendum' (Jeremy Thorpe, May 1970).

'I am not prepared to do that because I believe that the Parliamentary system which we have is quite capable of doing it' (Edward Heath, May 1970).

'I think it is right that it is the Parliament which should take the decision with a sense of full responsibility, with a sense that reflects national views and national interests' (Harold Wilson, May 1970).

Such unanimity among British party leaders is rare, to say the least. In 1970, the case against a referendum was, it seemed, beyond serious dispute: Britain had never used referenda and this was no time to begin; Parliament represented the people; if we started transferring sovereignty to the people, there would be no way of stopping it; we would then have to hold referenda on issues such as capital punishment (as they do in some American states) or divorce law reform (as they had done in Italy).

The case against referenda was put with such conviction and clarity by its advocates that few could have anticipated the undignified reversal that was to follow. Once they had made the switch, however, the advocates seemed able to argue their new case with similar conviction and a surprising intolerance towards their former view. Their reversal can be explained in the context of the prevailing political mood. Although the idea of a referendum eventually became an issue of principle, it did not start off as one. Its early proponents were all anti-marketeers: their justification for a referendum — sometimes implicit, more often explicit — was that the British people were on their side. They could not sway Parliament and were forced to appeal to the people. At that stage their policy was overtly pragmatic. Only later did it take on the character of a crusade for popular democracy. The metamorphosis began in the Labour Party.

Towards the end of 1971, Tony Benn, the leading advocate of a referendum on the EEC (and of referenda in general) became Labour Party chairman. An opponent of EEC membership, he used his new position to raise the issue frequently and to excite the interest of party workers and sympathisers. President Pompidou's announcement that the French people were to be allowed to vote on the question of enlarging the EEC won Benn more support for his campaign. In March 1972, the National Executive Committee of the Labour Party formally asked the Parliamentary Labour Party to reconsider its position on a referendum. The campaign was gathering momentum and, from then on, was unlikely to be stopped. The arguments in favour of a referendum were now much more concerned with the intrinsic merits of public consultation, full-hearted consent, widening the democratic base, and so on, than with opposition to the EEC. The device was becoming more important than the result.

In 1972, the Parliamentary Labour Party supported a splinter group of the Conservative Party in Parliament on an amendment that called for a referendum before entry. Although the amendment failed, it left Labour's leaders in an ambiguous and embarrassing position; until then they had been against a referendum; for tactical reasons they had now supported one; they were hopelessly divided on the issue.

By the time that Britain entered the EEC on 1 January 1973, the majority view in the Labour Party was solidly anti-European and pro-referendum. The Labour Party refused to take its rightful place in the European Parliament at Strasbourg; the trade unions would not co-operate in the formation of the EEC's social and industrial policy in Brussels. In some ways only one half of Britain had actively joined the

EEC. Meanwhile, British public opinion was still strongly anti-European and becoming increasingly pro-referendum. And the Conservative government was battling with an alarming rate of inflation, decreasing public support and growing industrial unrest.

The 'miners' general election' of February 1974 saw the Labour Party's new official policy on the referendum enshrined in its manifesto. If returned to office, a Labour government would renegotiate Britain's terms of EEC membership; it would place the new terms before the country to decide — either by a referendum or a general election — whether Britain should remain in the EEC or withdraw. Even Labour's pro-marketeers had grudgingly assented to that policy as a means of maintaining party unity. If Labour won the election, therefore, a referendum was now almost certain. After twelve years of trying to enter the EEC it was now a distinct possibility that Britain would withdraw after only twelve months of membership.

The new minority Labour government started its renegotiations almost immediately. Interrupted only by the October election, talks with the EEC continued throughout 1974. Public opinion was now firmly in favour of a referendum and, since the talks were clearly achieving *some* changes to Britain's original terms, it now seemed certain that a referendum would indeed be held. This was confirmed by Harold Wilson on 23 February 1975, and by the House of Commons on 10 April, after a debate that ranged widely over constitutional questions that had not been discussed for decades. Andrew Duff, in Chapter 6, discusses some of these issues and examines their implications.

In March, the Cabinet had accepted, by sixteen votes in favour to seven against, the renegotiated terms. Its view was endorsed by a free vote of the House of Commons on 9 April: 396 MPs voted in favour of continued membership of the EEC, 170 voted against. A bare majority of Labour MPs had voted against continued membership, but the Labour government's position was final: 'Her Majesty's Government have decided to recommend to the British people to vote for staying in the Community' (Harold Wilson, in the official referendum leaflet distributed to all voters).

The campaign leading up to the referendum on 5 June was a curious affair. In the first place, there was the unprecedented spectacle of Cabinet Ministers, by special permission of the Prime Minister, taking opposite points of view. In the second place, the two camps, represented by two officially sponsored bodies — Britain in Europe and the National Referendum Campaign — comprised what in normal times would have been the most unlikely coalition of personalities and politicians. On the pro-market side was an impressive line-up of prominent Conservative, Liberal and Labour politicians; on the anti-market side were prominent Labour politicians, less prominent Conservatives and Liberals, Communists, National Front leaders and Ulster Unionists. In Chapter 4, Dipak Nandy describes the way in which the media handled this unique situation in the light of the respective campaign strategies.

On the whole, the opposing Cabinet Ministers were polite to one another during the campaign. Other adversaries were not so polite, but there was surprisingly little acrimony. It augured well, for this was to be the public's decision, not the leaders': both sides had to accept the majority verdict of the people. And both sides did, the pro-marketeers with alacrity, the anti-marketeers with grace. Moreover, nearly all of them accepted the verdict as *final*. In Chapter 5, Martin Collins's analyses of the voting figures bear out the remarkable consistency in both the turnout and the direction of voting in different counties and among different demographic groups.

We do not pretend to understand all the fluctuations of public opinion or government postures on this issue over the past fifteen years and before. Some are explainable by the politics of the period, some by the economic circumstances, some by the prevailing national mood. Some are inexplicable. We do know, however, that on 5 June 1975 the British people finally decided an issue that politicians had been grappling with since the war. The consent accorded by the public to British membership of the EEC was not quite 'whole-hearted', but it was, at least, convincing.

2 MOVEMENTS IN THE PUBLIC MOOD: 1961-75
James Spence

'In my experience politicians suffer from a mild kind of schizo-phrenia about opinion polls. Of course they are omnivorously read at Westminster as well as round the corner in the two Party Head-quarters in Smith Square. Yet in his public statements about them the politician — especially when the polls have made an adverse prediction — tends to express a lordly disdain for their accuracy; and if the election results confirm their predictions, he begins to talk darkly about the malignant influence the pollsters exert on the mind of the electorate.'[1]

Crossman's views on the impact of opinion polls on Westminster apply most accurately to the period from the mid-sixties to the early seventies. Things were different, however, when the EEC was formed, chiefly because there were fewer polls. At that time, schizophrenia could have been applied equally to the political commentators and pundits who did what the polls did later: they made predictions about election results that were sometimes wrong but never ignored. When the EEC first became a political issue in Britain, some fifteen years ago, the occasional opinion poll published in the press was regarded with circumspection, if not outright suspicion. But the few that did appear were probably read as omnivorously as Crossman suggests. At that time, however, there was a lordly disdain for public opinion itself. Certainly it was not widely regarded by politicians as a key factor in major public decisions, let alone the decisive factor it was eventually to become.

The media, and particularly the press, played a prominent part in establishing the importance of public opinion on the EEC issue by funding and publishing regular opinion polls from 1961 onwards. The media's motives are not clear: proprietorial bias almost certainly played a part; so did the newsworthiness of Party disagreements; a desire for popular participation in political issues may also have played a part. Whatever the motives, however, we are indebted to the press and the pollsters for the wealth of poll data about the EEC on which we can draw. It not only provides a record of public opinion from the first negotiations in 1961 to the final confirmation in 1975. In many

18

cases. too, it helps to explain changes in the public mood, and to illuminate the possible causes of the change.

Macmillan's initiative (1961-3)

The 1961 polls showed the British public as unaware of the Common Market and its possible effects on Britain. Indeed, if we look back briefly to September 1957, shortly after the EEC was set up, many people in Britain were under the impression that Britain was already a member, and the majority had not even heard of the EEC.[2] By early 1961, the situation had changed little. The debate on European unity had only recently been rekindled in the Cabinet and in the inner circles of government by Macmillan's memorandum 'The Grand Design', whose aim was to secure a real unity of the Western half of a divided Europe 'thus returning to the concepts which had inspired the founding fathers of the European Movement nearly fourteen years before'.[3]

Nevertheless, the polls were already measuring not only public awareness of the EEC but public attitudes to Macmillan's EEC initiative. They were also continuing their regular measurements of public support for Macmillan and for his government in general. It would have been surprising if the two sets of measurements had not been related in some way — and they were. From mid-1960 to early 1962, Macmillan and his government lost more and more public support as the pay pause continued and the rate of inflation increased to 8 per cent. Simultaneously opposition to the government stance on the EEC rose from 12 per cent to over 25 per cent. But the relationship between public support for Macmillan's government and approval of its EEC initiative weakened and disappeared between June 1962 and the end of the year. After the July 1962 government reshuffle, support for the EEC increased and the gap between supporters and opponents widened. Government popularity remained steady.

Examining the Gallup poll data from the time of the Macmillan government's formal application for EEC membership in July 1961 — when Gallup found more people undecided (41 per cent) than either for (37 per cent) or against (23 per cent) — to the end of 1963, we find that support for membership fluctuated as events unfolded but stayed broadly within the 40 per cent to 50 per cent band. The main change was the steady hardening of opinion against EEC entry as more people joined the opposition from the ranks of the undecided.[4]

The reasons people gave for supporting membership tended to be vague and general — 'it'll be good for trade' — matters of faith, not fact. Rather more specific criticisms were voiced by people opposed to

Chart 1. Public Opinion during the Macmillan Initiative (Gallup Poll Quarterly Averages) 1961-3

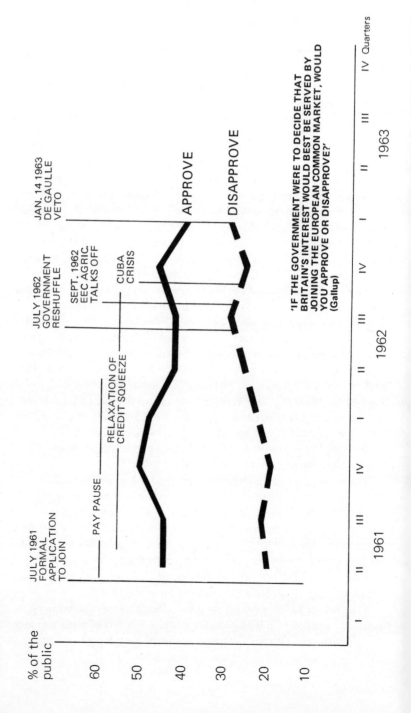

membership, who wished to stay with the Commonwealth and have
nothing to do with the EEC, who feared unemployment (which was
increasing) and high prices (which were getting higher).[5] In October
1962, towards the end of fifteen months of negotiations on the British
application, Gallup presented a sample of voters with a list of possible
effects of EEC membership. More than half of the sample nominated
food price increases and the availability of a wider choice of goods as
likely consequences, 42 per cent an increase in exports and 35 per cent
an increase in industrial efficiency. But then the British public still
thought they had never had it so good; that the Commonwealth would
continue to be a strong association with Britain at its head; that Britain
could teach 'the Europeans' something about trade and democracy.
Yes, members of the public would have to put up with higher prices,
but increased trade would enable them to afford it. Doubts were
appearing: the pay pause, continued modest growth, accelerating
inflation, industrial unrest, rising unemployment, problems with the
nations of the emerging independent Commonwealth, government
instability — all indicated problems ahead. But the public and the
government were only just beginning to suspect how intransigent
these problems would eventually become.

General de Gaulle's first veto on 14 January 1963 removed the
EEC issue, temporarily, from the political agenda. By then political
analysts had learned something about public opinion on the EEC
issue. It was volatile, mainly because most people knew and cared
little about the issue and the arguments. They therefore tended to
follow the lead of the political party they supported, or to accept
government policy, or to believe the newspaper they read.[6] Government policy (as relayed by the media) was probably the most influential of the three factors.

The Common Market stances of the political parties differed. The
Conservative government was firmly committed to joining if terms to
safeguard the Commonwealth and agriculture could be agreed. The
Labour Party under Gaitskell was less committed: the 1962 Labour
National Conference approved a resolution critical of the government's
EEC stance, seeking to impose stiff conditions on membership, but not
against membership on principle. The Liberals, as always, were committed pro-Europeans. According to poll data collected towards the end
of 1961, the public was moderately aware of each party's stance.

The governing party's policy was more visible than that of either
opposition party (more people were aware of the Conservatives' EEC
stance), and this visibility increased. Government initiatives were to

Perceived stance on EEC issue (September 1961)

	Conservative Party %	Liberal Party %	Labour Party %
In favour	49	30	24
Against	9	5	18
Undecided	18	13	24
No opinion/don't know	24	52	34

Source: Gallup.

become more frequent and more public in the ensuing months.

Kitzinger (1973)[7] suggests that newspapers had no effect on public views about EEC membership. Evidence from January 1963 polls suggests otherwise. Readers of the *Daily Express* and the *Daily Herald* showed much lower support for entry than the national average, reflecting the different editorial stances of these two papers from the stance of the rest of the press. Comparison between these papers and others with similar political leanings (such as the *Daily Mail* and the *Daily Mirror*, both pro-market but Conservative and Labour respectively), suggests that the differences were due partly to factors other than the political complexions of their readers. In later years, however, the relationship between newspaper readership and views on the EEC seems to disappear.[8]

Support for Common Market membership by newspaper readership (January 1963)

		% for Britain's joining the EEC
All electors		44
Readers of:	*Daily Express*	36
	Daily Mail	58
	Daily Herald	34
	Daily Mirror	47
	The Times	58
	(Manchester) Guardian	55
	Daily Telegraph	58

Source: NOP.

The polls showed that the antis tended to be concentrated among the poorer working class, women and older groups, to whom the threat of price increases was likely to be critical. Middle class groups, men and younger groups, tended to be more in favour. In the coming years this demographic pattern persisted, despite the movements of party supporters.

Wilson's initiative (1965-70)

Labour's election success in 1964 was heralded by many commentators as the beginning of a new era, of the 'modernisation of Britain'. And this mood was largely maintained until after the election of March 1966. During this time, opposition to Common Market entry gradually evaporated to around 15 per cent. Support soared to 70 per cent. It was the beginning of a period of euphoria — a very short period as it turned out. Satisfaction with the government's record and with Harold Wilson's first spell as Prime Minister rose (with a slight setback in mid-1965). Average earnings were increasing by about 7 per cent a year and prices were increasing by about 4½ per cent.

Several factors seem to have been involved in the shift of public opinion in favour of joining the EEC. All three major parties, for instance, now supported negotiation for entry, and their support must have influenced some people. People may have been reacting, too, to the poor balance of payments, and looking to the EEC to boost Britain's flagging trade. They may have felt, moreover, that the EEC did not mean a merging of nations and nationalities, but a loose configuration of largely independent trading states. As the Rhodesian crisis gathered momentum, the British public may have started to feel more sceptical about the Commonwealth as a realistic alternative to the EEC.

All these factors may have had an effect, but the major influence on public opinion was probably Wilson's espousal of the idea. If his popularity was to decline, the overwhelming support for EEC membership was likely to slip away. And in 1967 it did. After the March 1966 general election the economic situation got worse; the Government applied a credit squeeze and measures to regulate sterling outflows during the summer of 1966. Average earnings dropped; by the first quarter of 1967 they were increasing at an annual rate of only 2¾ per cent while prices rose at 3¾ per cent. The economic measures of summer 1966 were not well received by the public. Both the Government's and Mr Wilson's popularity fell sharply, and although this was not accompanied by an immediate fall in support for EEC membership, by May 1967, when Britain's formal application was submitted, public

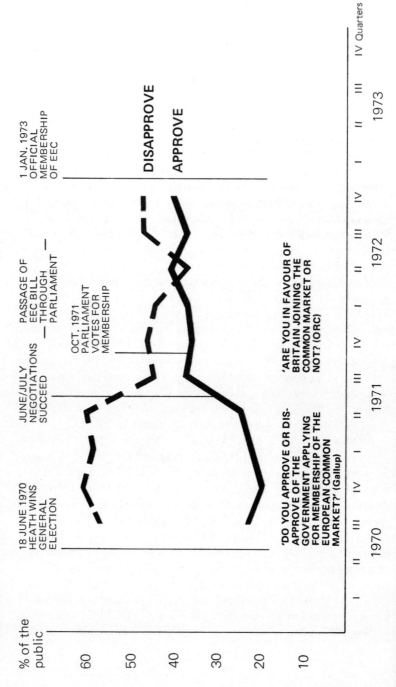

Chart 2. Public opinion during the Wilson initiative (Gallup Poll Quarterly Averages, 1964-8: NOP 1969-70) 1964-70

support for EEC membership had fallen away. The disenchantment
was experienced by both Conservative and Labour supporters, although
it was more marked among the former, as Berrington has shown.[9]

Percentage gap between supporters and opponents of Britain's entry
to the EEC

	All electors	Conservative supporters	Labour supporters
October 1965	+ 28%	+ 28%	+ 26%
November 1966	+ 41%	+ 43%	+ 38%
November 1967	− 6%	− 17%	+ 12%

Source: NOP.

Associated with the dramatic decline in support for Britain's entry was
a growing belief that membership would aggravate the price inflation
(particularly for food items) without compensating for the increase by
offering greater choice of European goods or jobs. Gallup shows a large
increase in the proportion of the public expecting food price rises on
membership from October 1962 to April 1967. (See table overleaf.)

Price inflation caused widespread and consuming fears. The run on
sterling and its devaluation in November 1967 may have been critical in
confirming the trend towards opposition to EEC membership. But de
Gaulle's intransigence must also have helped. And the public's lack of
knowledge about the EEC and what it involved is likely to have meant
that in general its response to such factors and events was intuitive
rather than informed. The debate, such as it was, pointed out the key
issues of membership without providing the public with the information it needed to evaluate them.

Even in times of considerable change, however, some patterns remain constant: in 1966-7 as in 1961-3, opponents of market membership were more numerous among women, the old, and working class
groups; men, the young and middle class groups were more in favour
than the average. (See table overleaf.)

de Gaulle's second veto in late 1967 did not remove Britain's
application to join the EEC from the negotiating table altogether.
Interest, however, did not revive in Britain until he resigned the
Presidency in May 1969. The British public seemed to believe that his
resignation would make it easier for Britain to join the EEC, though

Some perceived effects of EEC membership 1962-7

	October 1962	April 1967
% thinking EEC membership would . . .		
Raise food prices	58	76
Cause unemployment	28	21
Reduce the power of parliament	19	18
Make the Commonwealth collapse	13	22
Take away our (political) independence	28	22
Raise exports	42	38
Increase industrial efficiency	35	28
Give us a wider choice of goods in the shops	54	38
Give us a chance of going abroad for a job	31	20
Raise our standard of living	23	19
Make Britain's voice more powerful in international affairs	23	26

Source: Gallup.

Profile of supporters of EEC membership (June 1966)

	% in favour
All electors	66
Men	72
Women	60
Middle class (ABC1)	77
Skilled working (C2)	68
Unskilled working (DE)	54
21-34 year olds	74
35-54 year olds	69
55 year olds or over	58

Source: ORC.

most were still hostile to it in the ensuing months.[10] Throughout 1969, public support for membership gradually declined and, by March 1970, after publication of the Government's white paper on the costs of membership,[11] it had fallen to 22 per cent.[12] The *Express* was quick to splash the poll findings on its front page, demonstrating that the Great British public was saying 'No' to Europe. The pro-market *Mail* discreetly printed its similar findings on page two.

What brought about the great downturn in support? At the emotional level, in the face of two European rebuffs, the British public had to believe that Britain could go it alone, partly to restore self-confidence, partly to save face and partly as a defiant reaction to having been scorned. At the political level, most had come to accept that Britain would not lead the EEC, nor indeed be *primus inter pares*. In November 1969, 55 per cent of the public endorsed the statement that Britain would 'take a back seat' to some other EEC country (such as France or Germany).[13] Eight years earlier, only 33 per cent had agreed to that. More generally, fewer people then considered closer political relationships with EEC countries a good thing. At the economic level, the expectation that membership would bestow benefits and opportunities on Britain had gradually given way to a pervasive fear of higher prices: in November 1969, 72 per cent of the public thought that food prices would rise steeply; nine per cent had thought so in September 1961.[14] And 42 per cent thought that prices of other goods would rise steeply; 5 per cent had thought so in 1961. At the financial level, Britain's confidence had been sapped by the balance of payments and sterling problems that the country had experienced (and had been reminded of endlessly by the media) since 1964. In apparent recognition of this, fewer people in November 1969 than in September 1961 were prepared to endorse the removal of all trade barriers with the EEC (51 per cent against 61 per cent). And fewer people thought it a good thing to remove 'eventually all subsidies and other protection to industries, like agriculture' (39 per cent in 1961, 28 per cent in 1969).[15]

In retrospect, the most striking feature of Wilson's initiative to join the EEC was the disappearance during the period of the popular base for his action. The Labour Government had lost support and was to lose the general election in June 1970. But the decline in public support for membership of the EEC was overwhelming. From a starting point of eagerness and enthusiasm, the public had steadily moved in the direction of sullen resentment of the EEC. The next round of negotiations was to begin in an atmosphere of widespread public opposition.

Heath's initiative (1970-72)

After his unexpected rise to power, Heath swiftly restarted negotiations
for the entry of Britain and other countries. The outgoing Labour
Government had left a furiously inflating economy, by the standards of
the time, but average earnings were still ahead of prices. People knew
little about the EEC, regarded it as a low priority for government
action and were generally against membership, but resigned themselves
to the probability that Britain would join in the end. There was, according to the first of SCPR's three studies on public attitudes towards the
EEC, a

'. . . feeling that there is a conspiracy on the part of politicians,
media owners and big business to commit Britain to joining the
Common Market before the public has had a chance to appraise
the pros and cons to know precisely what is happening . . .'[16]

The same study, in 1971, identified a feeling among members of the
public that they did not know enough about the advantages and disadvantages of membership, and a demand for more information.
Among their needs was information about the EEC itself and about
how it compared with Britain. Asked to compare Britain with the
EEC countries on a variety of topics, a large proportion of the
sampled population could not even guess at answers. And those who
did were not always very accurate.[17]

Public evaluation of social and economic standards in Britain and the
EEC (Spring 1971)

	Thought Britain was better	Thought EEC was better
	%	%
Pensions	26	14
Family allowances	28	10
Paid holidays	13	34
Health service	79	2
Higher earnings	24	32
Higher standard of living	24	33
Lower level of unemployment	41	15

Source: SCPR.

Despite the element of chauvinism generated by this type of question, the table shows a growing realisation that Britain's economic position was extremely shaky in relation to that of most other EEC countries — a factor that was to prove increasingly important in the development of public opinion.

The Government's White Paper in July 1971 coincided with a change in the trend of public opinion. An NOP poll at the time[18] suggested that the White Paper and the accompanying press coverage had had the effect of rallying the supporters of the EEC, particularly from the ranks of the Conservative Party and among the elderly.

Approval of Britain's joining the Common Market at the time of the White Paper on EEC membership (July 1971)

	All	Interviewed prior to the publication of the White Paper (6-7 July)	Interviewed after publication of the White Paper (8-12 July)
	%	%	%
Approve	34	29	39
Disapprove	44	47	41
Don't know	22	24	20

NOP added:' This could be a sampling freak, yet in terms of age, class and sex and voting intention those contacted on Thursday (8 July) or later were not dissimilar to those contacted on Wednesday or before.'

Later in 1971 the polls indicated that support and opposition to entry were fairly balanced, but that there was a substantial and disconcertingly intractable proportion of 'don't knows'. Despite individual poll fluctuations about the norm, this general pattern held until Britain's entry in 1973.

Chart 3. Public opinion during the Heath initiative 1970-73 (Gallup and ORC)

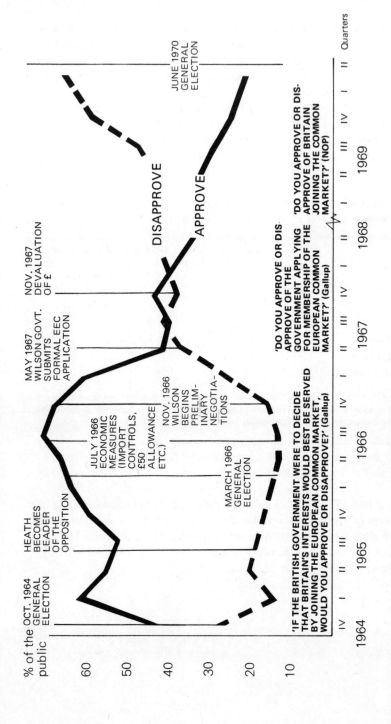

% of the
public

'IF THE BRITISH GOVERNMENT WERE TO DECIDE
THAT BRITAIN'S INTERESTS WOULD BEST BE SERVED
BY JOINING THE EUROPEAN COMMON MARKET,
WOULD YOU APPROVE OR DISAPPROVE?' (Gallup)

'DO YOU APPROVE OR DIS-
APPROVE OF THE
GOVERNMENT APPLYING
FOR MEMBERSHIP OF THE
EUROPEAN COMMON
MARKET?' (Gallup)

'DO YOU APPROVE OR DIS-
APPROVE OF BRITAIN
JOINING THE COMMON
MARKET?' (NOP)

DISAPPROVE

APPROVE

OCT. 1964
GENERAL
ELECTION

HEATH
BECOMES
LEADER
OF THE
OPPOSITION

JULY 1966
ECONOMIC
MEASURES
(IMPORT
CONTROLS,
£50
ALLOWANCE
ETC.)

NOV. 1966
WILSON
BEGINS
PRELIM-
INARY
NEGOTIA-
TIONS

MARCH 1966
GENERAL
ELECTION

MAY 1967
WILSON GOVT.
SUBMITS
FORMAL EEC
APPLICATION

NOV. 1967
DEVALUATION
OF £

JUNE 1970
GENERAL
ELECTION

Quarters

1964   1965   1966   1967   1968   1969

Change in overall views on EEC membership (October 1970 — July 1971)

| | % approving | | Relative change |
| | October 1970 | July 1971 | |
	%	%	%
All	24	34	+ 42
Men	30	41	+ 37
Women	19	28	+ 47
18-24	32	36	+ 13
25-34	29	37	+ 28
35-44	28	35	+ 25
45-54	26	37	+ 42
55-64	19	30	+ 58
65 +	16	27	+ 69
Conservative supporters	27	51	+ 89
Labour supporters	22	22	0
Liberal supporters	28	34	+ 21

Source: NOP.

The pre-referendum period (1973-5)

The public became rather more aware of the EEC's strengths and weaknesses in comparison with Britain's once Britain had joined. ORC showed that fewer people in 1973 than in 1971 believed that Britain had a higher standard of living than other EEC countries; more people believed that EEC countries had longer holidays, higher wages and more influence in the world than Britain; fewer believed that the cost of living was higher in EEC countries than in Britain.[19]

During 1973, however, the argument about membership went on; now it was about whether to stay in. The argument coincided with a period of high inflation and of increasing government unpopularity. History was repeating itself: growing hostility to the government was accompanied by growing hostility to membership of the EEC. Heath and his government tried desperately to convince a sceptical public that price inflation was not mainly due to the EEC but to world commodity price increases. Only the oil crisis at the end of the year allowed them to get the message across. But by then the disunity of the European communities had been demonstrated on at least two occasions.

Chart 4. Public opinion during the pre-referendum period (1973-5) (Gallup)

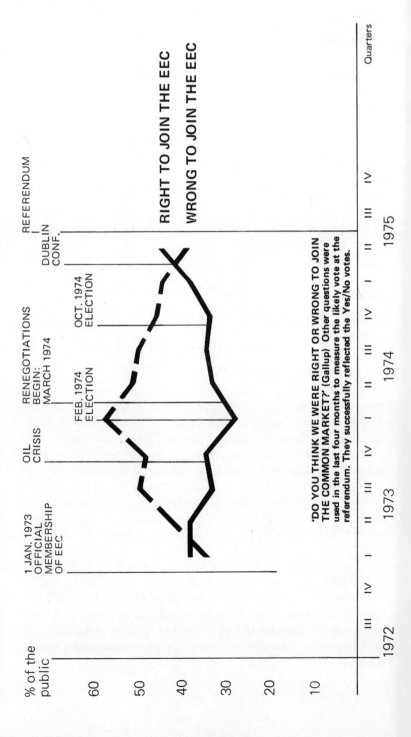

RIGHT TO JOIN THE EEC

WRONG TO JOIN THE EEC

'DO YOU THINK WE WERE RIGHT OR WRONG TO JOIN THE COMMON MARKET?' (Gallup) Other questions were used in the last four months to measure the likely vote at the referendum. They successfully reflected the Yes/No votes.

So it was Wilson's turn, when he was unexpectedly returned to office in February 1974, to inherit the atmosphere of public opposition to Britain's continued membership of the EEC.

The Labour Party's election manifesto in February 1974 stated that some kind of consultation with the people — either through a general election or through a consultative referendum — would be carried out on the promised renegotiation of the terms of British membership of the EEC: 'Thus the right to decide the final issue of British entry into the market will be restored to the British people.' At that time, prices were rising at an annual rate of about 13 per cent, average earnings at about 10 per cent. But people were now ready to accept that membership of the EEC was not the main contributor to the rise in the cost of living, and that renegotiation was an attractive alternative to leaving the community. Support for renegotiation grew during the summer of 1974, and by October more than two thirds of the public favoured this course. Their opinions on Britain's continued membership of the EEC could thus be suspended until the results of the renegotiations were known.

Public views on continued membership 1973-4

	January 1973 %	October 1974 %
We should stay in the Common Market on the present terms of entry	31	6
We should stay in but try to renegotiate the terms of entry	35 ⎫	53 ⎫
We should pull out but try to renegotiate the terms of entry	5 ⎭ 40	15 ⎭ 68
We should pull out of the Common Market altogether	15	16
Not answered/don't know	14	10

Source: ORC.

The key factor was clearly going to be the Government's recommendation arising from the renegotiation. Gallup asked the question: 'If the Government negotiated new terms for Britain's membership and they thought it was in Britain's interests to remain a member, how would

you vote then — to stay in or leave it?' Despite the fact that a majority
of the public at this time thought that Britain was wrong to have
entered the EEC, those who said they would support the Government's
recommendation outnumbered the proportion who said they would
not by 30 per cent. And this differential was to grow: by March 1975
it was 43 per cent. But the trend was accompanied by renewed support
for staying in on any grounds. By March 1975, a bare majority was
once again in favour of Britain's membership of the EEC.

The polls were still showing that the groups most opposed to EEC
membership comprised more than their expected proportions of the
old, the working class, the Scots, women and Labour supporters;
but young voters had now been added to the list. Gallup's analysis
of the combined pre-referendum surveys conveys the wisdom of
the pro-market campaigners in concentrating their attentions on
these groups (particularly working class women, the 18-24 year olds
and Scottish voters). What little change in public attitudes took place
between the end of March and referendum day was more than pro-
portionate among these groups.

Questions remain about how much information generally got through
to the public during the referendum campaign. Barry Hedges discusses
this in Chapter 3, but ORC, who found that only a minority felt well
informed on the issue, concluded that 'as an exercise of political
persuasion, the Common Market referendum campaign must be considered something of a flop'.[20]

Nevertheless, on the major issue of prices, the argument did seem

Items 'mainly to blame for increases in the price of things you buy in
the shops over the last three years' (1973-5)

	July 1973 %	June 1975 %
The Common Market	51	19
Worldwide increases in the price of food and raw materials	49	64
The trade unions	25	47
Manufacturers and businesses	21	16
Retailers and shopkeepers	15	13

Source: ORC.

finally to have been won by the pro-market lobby. Between July
1973 and June 1975 far fewer people persisted in blaming the EEC
for price inflation, and more blamed worldwide commodity price
increases and the trade unions' wage deals.[21]

On 5 June 1975, the public reacted as they had intimated they
might. By the conclusion of the Dublin conference in March 1975,
public support for membership had increased — and the number of
people who thought Britain was wrong to have joined had declined. By
the end of March, all the polls showed sizeable majorities planning to
vote 'yes'. These majorities fluctuated little up to polling day, despite
the range of parliamentary and party votes and messages that appeared
in the media in the final few months.

The evidence of the opinion polls over the years has shown an electorate conscious of its lack of information on many crucial issues,
inclined on the whole to be agnostic rather than stridently
opinionated in its basic attitudes, and waiting for a lead — not a
forelock-tugging, deferential one but an informed and informative
one from its traditional leaders in government. In the final stages of the
referendum campaign it became clear that no such lead would appear.
The Cabinet was divided, every party was divided, experts were
divided, television was 'balanced'. The 'facts' presented to the public
were mutually contradictory; the 'specialists' views' were often un-
specialised and emotionally loaded. Whether Britain should stay in the
EEC was a matter of opinion: not expert opinion but public opinion
after all.

References

1.   R. H. S. Crossman, 'Are the Political Pollsters Doing a Serious Job?
      Psephology between Social Science and Journalism', *Encounter*, XLI,
      No. 4, October 1973, p. 15.
2.   Social Surveys (Gallup Poll) Limited, *British Attitudes towards the
      Common Market 1957-71* (London: Gallup), August 1971, p. 4.
3.   H. Macmillan, *At the End of the Day 1961-1963* (London: Macmillan),
      1973, p. 4.
4.   Both Gallup and NOP have relevant data covering this period which show
      slightly different patterns. The different questions used probably account
      for this.
5.   Gallup *op. cit.* questions 81 and 82, and NOP as cited in F. Teer and
      J. Spence, *Political Opinion Polls* (London: Hutchinson), 1973, pp. 118-9.
6.   *NOP Political Bulletin*, January 1963, p. 4, and H. Berrington 'Public
      Opinion and the Common Market', paper given to the Universities
      Association for Contemporary European Studies (UACES) Seminar,
      March 1975, mimeo.
7.   U. Kitzinger, *Diplomacy and Persuasion* (London: Thames and Hudson),
      1973.

8. *NOP Political Bulletins*, July 1967, appendix and August 1967. Political affiliations and newspaper readership.

9. H. Berrington, *op. cit.*, appendix I gives a most useful table by party within demographic groups from analysis of NOP data on opinions about EEC membership.

10. *NOP Political Bulletin*, May 1969, and ORC *Britain and the Common Market: a summary of research* (London: Opinion Research Centre), February 1972, p. 26.

11. *Britain and the European Communities: an economic assessment*, Cmnd. 4289 (London: HMSO), 1970.

12. *NOP Political Bulletin*, March 1970.

13. Gallup, *op. cit.*, question 72.

14. *Ibid.*, question 76.

15. *Ibid.*, question 68.

16. J. Morton-Williams, *Attitudes towards the European Common Market: report on an exploratory study* (London: SCPR), P. 192, January 1971, p. (i).

17. B. Hedges and R. Jowell, *Britain and the EEC* (London: SCPR), 1971, pp. 18-20.

18. *NOP Political Bulletin*, July 1971, and cited in U. Kitzinger, *op. cit.*, p. 362.

19. ORC *mimeo*.

20. ORC *EEC Referendum: Second story* (London: Opinion Research Centre), ORC 47519, 6 June 1975, p. 1.

21. ORC, *EEC Referendum: Evening Standard special referendum survey* (London: Opinion Research Centre), ORC 47519, 5 June 1975, p. 5.

3 THE FINAL FOUR YEARS: FROM OPPOSITION TO ENDORSEMENT

Barry Hedges

We have seen in Chapter 2 the movement of public opinion during Britain's long courtship of Europe. In 1971, when there was every prospect that Britain would finally be allowed to join the EEC, SCPR undertook the first of three detailed studies of public attitudes towards Europe. Their object was not to duplicate the opinion polls but to examine a broader spectrum of public attitudes, opinions, hopes and fears. Though focused on the EEC, they looked also at Britain's place in the world, its economic performance, its relationship with the Commonwealth, and other matters of this kind that provided the context for the debate about Europe.

The change in attitudes during the final four years was dramatic. Early in 1971 we asked a representative sample of British electors how they would feel if Britain joined the EEC. Here are the replies:

	%	
Very pleased	4	28% pleased
Quite pleased	24	
Quite disappointed	28	52% disappointed
Very disappointed	24	
I'm not sure, it depends	20	

A little over four years later, British electors voted to stay in the community they had meanwhile joined, and we asked another sample of them how they felt about the result:

	%	
Very pleased	28	66% pleased
Quite pleased	38	
Quite disappointed	18	29% disappointed
Very disappointed	11	
I'm not sure	5	

In this chapter the three SCPR surveys — the two quoted above and another undertaken in 1974 — will be analysed to see what explanations can be found for this reversal of public opinion during the four years that preceded the referendum.

The first of these surveys involved personal interviews with 2,030 electors, selected by probability sampling methods and representative, within certain limits, of the entire British electorate at that time. The findings were set out in an SCPR report.[1]

The second survey, conducted in June 1974 after Britain had become an EEC member, followed much the same general method as the first survey, but with a smaller sample (1,326) and a modified questionnaire. It, too, was the subject of a report.[2] Because of the increasing prominence of the issue of devolution at that time, it was important to be able to look separately at the Scottish and Welsh results, and the proportion of interviews assigned to these countries exceeded their share of the population (the imbalance being adjusted during the analysis).

The third survey, in June 1975, was similar in general character to its predecessors, but there was one important difference. Instead of approaching a fresh sample, we reinterviewed the 1974 sample. This had the great advantage of allowing us to see the way in which individuals changed their attitudes — if they did change them — during the critical pre-referendum year, and thereby to carry out a more penetrating analysis of what actually happened. Of the 1,326 electors interviewed in 1974, 1,014 were successfully reinterviewed in 1975. Those already familiar with the 1974 survey report may notice small discrepancies between percentages given there and those quoted from it in the present chapter. This is because some of the analyses we now give have been based on the sample of 1,014 reinterviewed electors instead of on the original 1974 survey base of 1,326 electors. No separate report has been published on the 1975 survey, but a technical description of the methods used is available.[3]

These three surveys cannot by themselves provide a complete explanation of the change in the public mood from opposition to the endorsement of membership, but they illuminate certain aspects of that change. Their interpretation needs to take account of other knowledge, such as the opinion poll data summarised by James Spence in Chapter 2, and must be set within that context. In the following paragraphs, before dealing with the survey results themselves, we set down some broad impressions formed as we have worked through the survey material. They are all prompted by one or another of our findings, but in some cases we have gone beyond these to sketch out interpretations that necessarily have a subjective element.

By the beginning of the 1970s, the British public, always somewhat stand-offish in its relations with Europe, had settled sulkily into an anti-European posture. Britain had more than once made overtures to its prospective partners: but each time it had had its face slapped. We were *not* in favour of joining the EEC, as the opinion polls kept telling us.

SCPR's first survey, in 1971, reflected this, but also showed that opposition to the EEC was by no means as solid as the numbers implied. The anti ranks were swollen by a substantial number of adherents who neither knew nor cared much about the issue, but perhaps simply distrusted foreigners, or didn't like the upheaval that a change in the *status quo* would involve. The same survey also brought out clearly the conflict between the short and the long run. All the short-term arguments seemed against joining the EEC; most of all people anticipated, and feared, rising prices. But it was widely believed that in the long term EEC membership would prove to be an advantage. Would this be sufficient to justify the sacrifices that would have to be made? Many, even of those who believed in the long-run benefits, thought not. As our 1971 report pointed out, the dice were loaded towards the short-term: 'price increases are a painfully familiar phenomenon; economic growth is not.'

The ensuing period proved to be a difficult one for Britain. For a number of years there had been talk of economic crisis, but life didn't seem to have changed very much, and we had continued to become better off. But now the Macmillanerie of the late fifties — with material progress stretching to the far horizon — seemed to be letting us down. So did Wilsonian technology. Perhaps things weren't going to go on getting better after all? Meanwhile the Commonwealth was becoming more alien and less reliable as a source of support. Threatened, we felt that Europe might offer some kind of haven. 'The way the world is going, it is better for Britain to be in a larger community', said one of our respondents. 'We can't stand alone', echoed another.

After entry, opinion at first swung away from Europe. The idea of joining had not become popular, even though it had come to be more widely accepted, and it is not particularly surprising that there should have been an immediate reaction. But as time went by it didn't seem to be too bad after all. People had suspected that some pretty unpleasant things would happen pretty quickly, but on the whole they didn't. And some of those that did seemed to be attributable not to the EEC but to other forces: conspicuously, though not solely, Arab states

which were charging high prices for oil. So, even if we weren't too
keen to get in, why bother to get out? An important factor here was
the basic conservatism of the British public which resists change,
perhaps even when it *is* desirable. And when there isn't any solid
reason for changing, we vote for the *status quo*. In 1971 and 1972 the
status quo was outside Europe; in 1973 and beyond it was inside.

One of our respondents neatly summarised this point of view. He
was an anti-European who thought the referendum should have been
held years ago '. . . and we would never have gone in. But the British
people don't like change, so it was a foregone conclusion that we would
stay in. That's politics for you.' Some of the comments people made to
us also indicated a feeling that when you have started on something,
you shouldn't just give it up without a fair trial, for reasons both of
expediency and of principle:

'We have spent so much money on going in, it would be a complete
waste if we had to come out.'

'I don't think we could come out now without giving it a fair trial.'

'To come out was going to be more trouble than it was worth, and
could cost money that we cannot afford.'

'Having gone into the EEC it would have been a loss of dignity for
the country if we had said no.'

'If we had been asked in the first place I would have said no, but as
we are in we should stay in.'

One of the key arguments against entry had been the loss of sovereignty
entailed. The practical consequences of this were not easy to anticipate,
and many people felt that jealously preserving our autonomy would
serve Britain's interests less well than joining up with other people (not
necessarily Europe: the Commonwealth still evoked a response from
the public, and there was also the United States). Once inside, there
certainly were issues, some of them important, on which Britain's
policies and practices had to be aligned with those of the EEC. But
few of these were of a kind to catch the public imagination, and it
probably seemed to many that the consequences of loss of sovereignty
were not burdensome. Perhaps this view had been too easily formed,
since in so short a period the really testing problems might not yet

have occurred, but it is not easy to live in a state of perpetually reserved judgement, and we need not be surprised if people came to accept the situation in the absence of events to point them in the other direction.

There seemed to be a difference in the character of support for each side. Both sides had well-informed, dedicated protagonists. There was no lack of seriousness on the anti-market side: indeed, the more earnest anti-marketeers seemed to have a kind of passionate intensity that was not altogether matched on the other side, and this is reflected in our figures. It was as if entry into Europe was an indecent act that provoked indignation by its intrinsic nature rather than by any calculation of its consequences. But there was also, on the anti-market side, a disproportionate share of ignorance and indifference. Such support is not only of little value to the cause to which it attaches (unless the issue can be speedily brought to the point of a count of heads), but it is also vulnerable. It may opt out altogether, or defect to the other side — and this seems to have happened.

Reaching a decision

The information the 1975 survey provides about voting behaviour and about the differences in voting between different population groups is summarised by Martin Collins in Chapter 5, where it is linked to published data about the number of 'Yes' and 'No' votes cast in each English or Welsh county or Scottish region. All that is needed here, therefore, is a simple statement of the national results, both from the survey and from published vote counts; from these figures it can be seen how closely representative the survey was of the disposition of the electorate:

	GB total	England	Scotland	Wales
Proportion of votes cast:				
SURVEY				
For staying in the EEC	69	70	56	65
For leaving the EEC	31	30	44	35
PUBLISHED VOTE COUNTS				
For staying in the EEC	68	69	58	65
For leaving the EEC	32	31	42	35

Seventy-six per cent of our respondents claimed to have voted in the referendum. Leaving aside the possibility of false claims to have voted (it has been demonstrated in other surveys that such claims are some-times made), this proportion seems high in relation to the official turnout (65 per cent). But as Martin Collins shows in Chapter 5 this apparent discrepancy is largely due to differences in the way people *unable* to vote (or to be interviewed) are dealt with in the calculations.

When did people finally decide which way to vote? According to their replies, almost half of those who voted finally made up their minds at some time in 1975 itself:

	All voting %	
Before 1975	52	
January-April 1975	14	48% decided in
May 1975	14	1975
June 1975/at the referendum	20	

Women seem to have taken the decision later than men (56 per cent of the women who voted had finally made up their minds during 1975, compared with 37 per cent of the men). Non-manual workers tended to have reached their decision at a rather earlier date than manual workers:

	% deciding in 1975
Professional, managerial	32
Other non-manual	43
Skilled manual	51
Semi-skilled and unskilled manual	54

In view of the fact that the net swing during the period was towards Europe, it is not surprising that groups with a basically more 'anti' stance should have reached their final decision comparatively late.

The swing can be seen more clearly by comparing each person's voting behaviour with the attitudes to the EEC he expressed in the 1974 survey. Three main groups of people were identified at that time:

1. Those who were in favour of staying in ('pro'); most of these thought that attempts should be made to improve the terms of membership, and were designated *conditionally* pro', but for analysis here they have been merged with the very much smaller group who were pro without qualification.
2. Those who wanted to leave unless better terms were obtained ('conditionally anti').
3. Those who wanted to leave anyway ('anti').

Eighty-six per cent of the votes subsequently cast by the 1974 pro-marketeers were for staying in, and 14 per cent for leaving (perhaps because the changes made to the terms were thought insufficient). Among the second group, the conditional antis, the 'stay in' share of the vote was 55 per cent. Among the third group, the antis, it was 32 per cent. Since these antis had expressed their earlier view without qualification, those who voted to stay in (about one in three) had clearly changed their minds.

We can look at these results another way. What proportion *of the entire sample* voted consistently with its previous attitude? And what proportion inconsistently? It is not possible to give exact answers to these questions because many people said their attitude depended on the outcome of the renegotiation of terms, but the diagram overleaf summarises our knowledge. Cross-hatched blocks indicate consistent views: it will be seen that 55 per cent retained their 1974 allegiance (38 per cent remaining pro, 17 per cent remaining anti). Dotted blocks indicate those who did, or might have, changed their minds (19 per cent in all), while those who did not vote (24 per cent) are shown as un-shaded blocks. (A very small proportion who did not express a view in 1974 are omitted, so the percentage total is a little less than 100 per cent.)

Some further evidence of mind-changing, this time for the period *preceding* 1974, is provided by one of the questions in the 1974 survey. After being asked to summarise their attitude (pro, conditionally pro, conditionally anti or anti), respondents were asked if they had changed their view in the year or two prior to summer 1974; and, if so, what their previous position had been. Nineteen per cent claimed to have changed; 3 per cent did not say in what direction, but 16 per cent did,

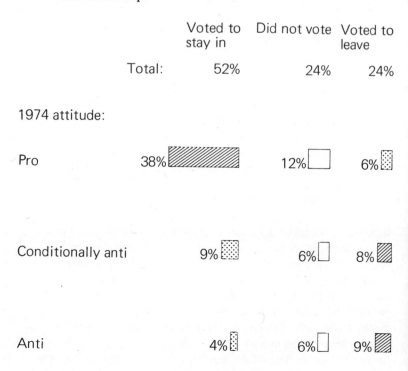

	Voted to stay in	Did not vote	Voted to leave
Total:	52%	24%	24%
1974 attitude:			
Pro	38%	12%	6%
Conditionally anti	9%	6%	8%
Anti	4%	6%	9%

Figure 1

so that an analysis of movements is possible. If we take these 16 per cent as a new base of 100 per cent the sizes of the different groups changing in one direction or another can easily be compared (see table on page 45).

Two features stand out. First, the net movement was on the whole in a direction favourable to the EEC; 54 per cent of these attitude changers finished up conditionally pro or pro, though only 42 per cent had so begun. Second, there is a marked movement away from the extremes towards the middle. Only 15 per cent now had a view which needed no qualification about terms of entry, whereas no less than 65 per cent had previously held such a view.

The period in respondents' minds may or may not have extended back before the date of entry (January 1973). We know from the opinion polls that there was a fairly even balance of opinion immediately prior to entry, but after that feelings swung for a considerable

	Pro	CHANGING TO:		Anti	Total
		Conditionally pro	Conditionally anti		
CHANGING FROM:	%	%	%	%	%
Pro	—	12	12	1	25
Conditionally pro	1	—	10	6	17
Conditionally anti	—	11	—	7	18
Anti	—	30	10	—	40
TOTAL	1	53	32	14	100

time against the EEC. It was generally believed in early 1974 that a referendum might well take Britain out of Europe, and our survey, conducted in the summer of that year, indicated that the tide might be turning back in Europe's favour. Jowell and Spence, the authors of the 1974 report, were obliged to be cautious since the renegotiated terms were not yet known, but they expressed the belief that if the government were to recommend remaining in the EEC, that recommendation would be accepted by the public. Subsequent events confirmed this: it was after the Prime Minister announced the renegotiated terms and reaffirmed the government's view at the Dublin Conference in March 1975 that there occurred the final pro-EEC swing that ensured Britain's continued membership.

It is not surprising, then, that our 1974 respondents should have appeared to be moving towards Europe rather than away from it. Their rather more marked movement from unqualified to qualified opinions probably reflects the increasing debate about renegotiation of the terms: people had become more conscious that this was happening and had less need to commit themselves to absolute views.

It will be helpful in studying the results of our three surveys to bear in mind the points of time at which they were undertaken and their relationship to the general movement of opinion throughout the period, summarised here from Chapter 2.

Opinion was favourable to Europe throughout most of the sixties, but towards the end of the decade the public's mood became markedly anti. This was still the prevailing feeling at the time of our first survey in February 1971 (and had been so for a couple of years): it showed 29 per cent pro, 52 per cent anti, with 19 per cent having no opinion either way. But it also showed that the situation could not be regarded as stable, and it was not long afterwards (in the late summer of 1971) that there was a sudden marked swing back towards the EEC. The balance of opinion became fairly even and stayed so until entry on 1 January 1973.

After entry, as already noted, there was a reaction, and opinion again became anti for the next year and a half. It seems to have begun to swing towards pro in summer 1974, when our second survey pointed to a renascence of pro feeling. But this did not really get under way until the Dublin conference in March 1975, when the final pro mood was established that lasted till the referendum and beyond it to the date of our third survey.

Party support and voting behaviour

It seems reasonable to assume that voting in the referendum would bear some relationship to party support in elections. For many, party loyalty and feelings about the EEC would have been in conflict. It is not the aim of this report to track changes in the degree of support for the major parties through the entire period. But it is germane to look briefly at the political background during 1974 and the first half of 1975; during the later part of this period, which included two general elections, the referendum campaign was under way. In our analysis we shall be able to use the fact that our 1974 and 1975 surveys were based on the same people to look at the pattern of changing loyalties at the individual level as well as at net shifts in party support.

There are four basic sets of responses to consider:

	Voted Feb. 1974	Voted Oct. 1974	Summer 1975: 'Would vote tomorrow'	Usually support
	%	%	%	%
Conservative	30	32	38	33
Labour	35	38	35	39
Liberal	17	13	10	12
SNP	2	2	2	1
Plaid Cymru	*	*	1	*
Communist	*	*	*	*
Other/refused to say/don't know	4	2	9	4
Didn't vote/wouldn't vote	12	12	5	N/A
None/no party	N/A	N/A	N/A	10

* = less than 0.5 per cent

The table shows the peak achieved by the Liberals in February 1974, declining in October and still falling in summer 1975 — apparently to a level below that of 'usual' support for the party. The Labour Party improved its position in October, but, as often happens with the party in power, then lost potential votes.

The analysis can be extended by seeing what degree of consistency in voting there was between February and October 1974. The table below shows what the pattern was. The figures shown are per 1,000 electors, not percentages, and omit 237 electors who did not vote on either or both occasions.

| | February 1974 | | | |
	Conservative	Labour	Liberal	Other
October 1974				
Conservative	248	15	21	1
Labour	11	287	42	2
Liberal	18	14	82	—
Other	3	4	1	14

It will be seen that if we treat 'others' for convenience as a single party, of these 763 voters 631 (83 per cent) voted the same way at each round. There was little Conservative ↔ Labour switching, and of similar extent in both directions. Slightly more Conservative ↔ Liberal switching can be seen, again equally in both directions. But the Liberal ↔ Labour interchange is more one-sided, the Liberals losing to Labour in October many more of their February votes than they gained in return. The implication of these figures is that the Liberal vote in February owed more to disaffected Labour supporters than to straying Conservatives. If the 'usual' party support of these switching voters is examined, it is found that of the 42 Liberal-to-Labours, 25 usually supported Labour, 3 Conservative and 7 Liberal (7 having no fixed allegiance); and of the 21 Liberal-to-Conservatives, 12 usually supported the Conservatives, 1 Labour and 5 Liberal (3 having no fixed allegiance).

The simplest way to look at the relationship between election and referendum voting is to consider the October 1974 election results alone. There is a striking difference between the three main party voting groups. The referendum voting of each was as follows.

| | General election: October 1974 | | | |
	Conservative %	Labour %	Liberal %	Non-voters %
Referendum:				
Voted to stay in	70	42	62	28
Voted to come out	14	34	21	16
Did not vote	16	24	17	56

Note: supporters of smaller parties are omitted.

The column on the far right shows the behaviour of those who did not vote in October 1974. It will be seen that over half of them did not vote in the referendum either. This 'apolitical' group constitutes 8 per cent of the total sample.

The number of people not voting varies from one general election to another. Chapter 5 shows that a substantial number of failures to vote are of an almost fortuitous character, resulting from changes of address or other circumstances similarly having no direct relation to views about exercising the franchise or about particular political issues. It is likely that there will be some electors who never vote at all. But there will be others who usually vote, but on occasions feel, perhaps because of the particular issues current at the time, that they would prefer to abstain. The composition, as well as the magnitude, of the non-voting element is thus likely to change from one election to another. It is of interest to see whether the people who did not vote in the February 1974 election did or did not vote in the October election. By cross-analysis, we find that 83 per cent voted in both elections, 7 per cent voted on neither occasion, 5 per cent voted only in February and 5 per cent voted only in October. Thus, out of every twelve who did not vote in February, seven did not vote in October either. It also appears that non-voters at the February election were a little more pro-European in attitude than were non-voters in October (see table on page 49).

The sample bases for this analysis are small (118 for February and 116 for October), but the elections were on very different issues and it is not surprising that there should be resulting differences in the character of abstentions.

		February 1974 non-voters %	October 1974 non-voters %
Referendum vote:	stay in	34	28
	leave	13	16
	did not vote	53	56

How much did people care?

The EEC has never been the public's chief preoccupation. As our 1974 survey showed, it took third place in a list of five issues, behind 'the power of trade unions in Britain' and well outstripped by 'price rises and inflation'. Unemployment and devolution came lower down the scale, presumably because they directly affect only minorities. In the same survey, the EEC was rarely mentioned when respondents were asked to name 'the most serious problem facing Britain today'.

But although it has never been *the* issue, it has been regarded by most people as a matter of real importance. And over the period covered by our surveys (1971-5) the EEC became progressively more important in the public's view. It is difficult to show satisfactory trend figures because of variations in the questions used. But if we divide the population into two groups at the mid-point of the attitude scale used on each occasion we find the following pattern:

	% attaching importance (above mid-point)
1971	64
1974	72
1975	87

One of the most significant findings of the 1971 survey had been that supporters of entry into the EEC almost all thought the issue an important one, whereas opponents of entry included many who thought the issue unimportant. It was this, together with a similar finding relating to levels of knowledge, that sounded one of the first warnings to those who relied too much on the simple count of heads 'for' and 'against' that the opinion polls provided: while opponents of entry were more numerous, a substantial part of their support came from a section of the public which did not attach much importance to the issue, and was not very well informed about it.

This group was clearly vulnerable to attack, as an analysis of the change between 1971 and 1974 shows. The importance of the issue was measured, in both surveys, on a seven-point scale, with 7 denoting greatest importance and 1 least. Here are the results for the two surveys, each figure being expressed as a percentage of the total sample for that year. The change between the years is shown in the third and sixth columns:

	Pro attitude			Anti attitude		
	1971 %	1974 %	Change	1971 %	1974 %	Change
Degree of importance attached:						
7 (High)	11	16	+ 5	15	17	+ 2
6	3	12	+ 9	4	7	+ 3
5	8	10	+ 2	5	4	− 1
4	4	8	+ 4	8	5	− 3
3	1	4	+ 3	6	4	− 2
2	1	2	+ 1	3	2	− 1
1 (Low)	1	2	+ 1	11	5	− 6
	29	54		52	44	

As we have noted earlier, the proportion holding a 'pro' view increased from 29 per cent to 54 per cent during this period. Part of the gain came from the group who in 1971 took a neutral position (omitted from the table): many of these believed the issue to be important, but did not know which side of the argument to adopt; they tended subsequently to form a pro rather than an anti view. But other pro gains were at the direct expense of the antis — and particularly of that group which rated the issue as one of very little importance. Because the 1971 and 1974 surveys — unlike 1974 and 1975 — used different samples, we cannot know for certain just what the pattern of transfers was: we can only observe the end result, but the above inferences from it seem reasonably certain.

In 1975 the tendency for a small rump of antis to regard the issue as unimportant seems to have persisted: nearly three quarters of votes cast by respondents who thought it 'not at all important' were for leaving the EEC.

The conclusions of the preceding paragraphs at first sight appear to conflict to some extent with those drawn by some commentators from the polls. Kitzinger,[4] for example, commenting on ORC data for 1971-2, points to a pattern 'that persisted throughout the series: those who felt very strongly opposed to entry always outnumbered those who felt less strongly opposed; while those who felt very strongly in favour of entry were always outnumbered by those who did not feel so strongly in favour'. The impression that might be gained from this is that it was the pro ranks (if either) that were swollen by the adherence of those more indifferent to the issue.

In fact, it can be shown both from our surveys and the polls that *strength of feeling* about the issue and *beliefs about its importance* were by no means synonymous. For example, half of those in our 1971 survey who attached the lowest level of importance to the issue nevertheless expressed a strong attitude about it. To be strongly in favour (or against) does not necessarily imply that the issue is believed to be important. Similarly, someone who believes it to be of great importance may not take up an extreme position for or against (he may, for example, feel insufficiently sure which of the two is the better course).

Kitzinger observed that the phenomenon he was commenting on became less marked with time (during the 1971-2 period). That trend seems to have continued, since by 1975 both pros and antis described the strength of their views in similar terms:

		Had voted to stay in %	Had voted to leave %
Felt:	very strongly	49	50
	quite strongly	35	33
	not very strongly	12	15
	not at all strongly	4	2

But the pros were much more inclined to think the issue important:

		Had voted to stay in %	Had voted to leave %
It mattered:	a great deal	73	49
	a fair amount	22	28
	not very much	4	17
	not at all	—	4
	no opinion, not stated	1	2

These replies show a considerable degree of polarisation of attitudes, which can be illustrated by means of Figure 2. Those voting to stay in are on the left half of the diagram, those voting to leave are on the right half. Each is divided into four groups according to the strength of feeling behind his vote. Feelings are strongest towards the outside edges of the diagram, weakest in the centre. All percentages are based on the total sample instead of on the number voting in each direction.

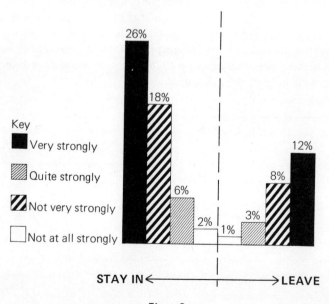

Figure 2

Once the generally larger numbers on the left-hand side of this diagram have been allowed for, it has a striking symmetry: as we have already noted, both sides claimed to have cast their votes with equal fervour. Still more striking is the extent to which views had polarised at this post-referendum stage. A possible explanation for this is that the act of voting in a particular direction can itself be a polarising mechanism: people may come out of a polling booth with certainty that they have done the right thing even if they were unsure in advance. But in fact a similar result was obtained in the 1974 survey:

	1974	1975
	Felt about the view they had expressed about EEC membership %	Felt about the way they had voted (based on voters only) %
Very strongly	53	49
Quite strongly	34	35
Not very strongly	11	13
Not at all strongly	2	3

So in spite of the uncertainty that characterised the EEC debate, of the changes of attitude and of the late stage at which many voting decisions were taken, most people seem to have felt fairly committed to the particular view they held at the time – at least by 1974: this may not have been true at earlier periods, when the issue was less prominent and less widely regarded as important.

It is of interest to note that political party support is less strongly expressed: of those who named a party they usually supported, about a third said they felt very strongly about this, compared with about a half who felt very strongly in support of their EEC stance.

What were the issues?

In view of the effort put into the campaign by the government and by the pro and anti factions – an effort of which the public was well aware – it is in some ways surprising that the general pattern of attitudes at the end was little different from that established long before. In 1971, people thought membership of the EEC would speed up the rate of price increases. They still thought so in 1975. In 1971, they thought membership would help to push wage rates up; similarly in 1975. They still felt in 1975 that membership meant having less say in our own affairs, but that from the defence point of view we were stronger in than out. As in 1971, they believed that the economic situation would be helped rather than hindered by membership. They were still fairly evenly divided about the effect of the EEC on employment. Nevertheless, there were a number of shifts of considerable interest.

Prices

In 1971, people expected that prices would rise faster if we joined the EEC than if we did not. This view, held by 81 per cent of the electorate, was among the most nearly unanimous in that survey. In 1974 people were more divided in their opinions, but many were blaming EEC membership as a contributory cause of the inflation that by then had reached an alarming rate. Two thirds of our respondents thought that prices had risen faster since entry than they would otherwise have done. And two thirds specifically mentioned the EEC when asked to pick from a list of six items those which were contributing to British food price rises. But other factors were also seen to be at work: even more named rises in world food prices than named EEC membership, while wage increases were also seen as an important contributor. These attitudes are correlated with subsequent voting behaviour in the referendum: those voting to stay in believed world food prices to be the main, and wage increases the secondary, cause of rises in British food prices, whereas those who voted to leave the EEC regarded membership as the main cause; predictably, perhaps, because of their generally more left-wing views, they also seemed a little more inclined to blame food manufacturers for increasing profits. (See table opposite.)

Many thus blamed price increases at least partly on membership; but rather fewer thought that *leaving* the EEC would slow down the rate at which prices were rising, a view to which 35 per cent subscribed.

One of the basic reasons for the fears about prices which have been a continuous feature of the debate was the realisation, shown by our 1971 survey, that many food prices were substantially higher in the Six. In consequence, rises were to be expected, especially for meat and butter (expected by about 85 per cent), milk and bread (65 per cent) and fresh fruit and vegetables (45 per cent). By 1974 the view that the prices of meat, milk, butter and bread were higher in other European countries than in Britain was less widely held than before, though still by a majority.

	Causes of rises in British food prices	Main cause	Main cause, according to:*	
			'Stay in' voters	'Leave' voters
	%	%	%	%
World food price rises	70	35	41	30
British membership of EEC	67	29	21	42
General wage increases	65	21	26	10
Manufacturers' increased profits	46	8	6	13
Shopkeepers' increased profits	28	3	2	2
Farmers' increased profits	13	1	1	1

* Note: non-voters are omitted.

Wages

About two in five electors in 1971 anticipated that Britain's entry into the EEC would help incomes to rise, while one in five expected it to spoil the chances of rises. The situation in 1975 was not very different, but such movement as there was tended to be favourable to the EEC.

	1971 %	1975 %
Membership helps wages to rise	37	40
Membership spoils the chance of wages rises	22	13
No effect; no view either way	41	47

Note: The 1971 question referred to *getting into* the EEC, the 1975 question to *staying in* it.

In 1974 a question was asked about the effect on wages of *leaving* the EEC, and this time many more (70 per cent) placed themselves in the third of the three categories. This may reflect greater uncertainty at that date, but more probably it is due to fewer people having a positive view about the consequences of leaving than about those of getting (or staying) in. A possible reason for the shift of attitudes in favour of the EEC on this issue is increased awareness of the higher wages that tend to be paid to workers in other European countries; another possibility is that people attributed to the EEC at least part of the rapid rise in British wages since entry.

Unemployment

Views about the effect of membership on unemployment tended in our surveys to be even more divided than views about its effect on wages. In 1975 the public split into three almost equal groups — those who thought unemployment would be increased by continuation in membership, those who expected it to be reduced, and those who either had no view or thought it would make no difference.

Four years before the position had not been so very different; such shift in attitudes as occurred between 1971 and 1975 appears to have been in the EEC's favour, since in the earlier year only 25 per cent expected unemployment to diminish as a result of joining. Among the fears current at the time was that Britain might be swamped by an influx of cheap labour, a view held by 40 per cent. Thus people tended to believe that jobs might become less secure (34 per cent thought this) as a result of entry. It was widely thought in 1971 that unemployment was higher in Britain than in the Six, but while higher prices there were expected to lead in due course to higher prices here, low unemployment was not expected to be similarly contagious.

General economic issues

In 1971 there was a good deal of uncertainty about whether Britain's standard of living had a faster or slower rate of growth than that of the Six. On the whole, the public believed it to be slower (33 per cent said this, while 24 per cent held the opposite view). But the great majority (77 per cent) thought that Britain had been 'getting poorer and poorer in comparison with most other industrial countries': the difference between this result and that reported in the preceding paragraph suggests that non-European countries (Japan? USA? the 'white Commonwealth'?) were the point of reference here.

By 1974 Britain's growth was seen by most people to be slower than that of other EEC countries: 54 per cent now endorsed this view, with only 19 per cent taking the opposite one. Even in 1971, however, people already regarded other European countries as dangerous economic rivals. A majority agreed that Britain would suffer from European competition after entry, but it was also believed that in the process we would somehow become 'more modern and efficient'. Few thought that entry would be a panacea for economic ills, and the public did not see membership of the EEC as the only way forward. Equal numbers (about 40 per cent) agreed and disagreed with the statement 'if we stay out of Europe, Britain's economy is more likely to improve', and only one in four was prepared to agree that 'if Britain does not join, most of us would be worse off than if she does'.

By 1974, the contrast between Britain's economic performance and Europe's had become widely recognised. Almost everyone believed that prosperity depended   on increased trade with other countries. But this had not led to any unanimity about the best means of improving the situation, and the public was fairly evenly divided on the question of whether it was better to be in or out of the EEC. But the public view then swung, during the year separating the two surveys, towards Europe, and in 1975 we found 43 per cent thinking that staying in the EEC would make our economic problems better, with only half as many believing it would make them worse. We do not know, however, whether the public's wry view about who was benefiting was also modified in the pre-referendum year. In 1971 there had been some optimism that Britain would benefit equally with the Six, but most of this had evaporated by 1974:

	1971 %	1974 %
Who benefits most?		
The Six	44	63
Britain	6	2
Both equally	31	16
Other responses	30	19

Political aspects

Throughout the debate, the issue of sovereignty and self-determination was prominent. Almost by definition, Britain would on entry lose the power to make at least some of the decisions formerly taken alone, and this was widely recognised by the public in 1971. Sixty-nine per cent, for example, agreed that after entry 'Britain won't be able to decide her own future'. Similarly, about three quarters believed Britain 'would have less say in her own affairs, if she joins the Common Market'. To say this, however, is not to conclude that people were necessarily concerned about the prospect. They may have felt that it was not, in practice, of great importance. This seemed to be implied by responses to another 1971 question, which showed an almost equal division of opinion between those who thought that our interests could be better protected outside the EEC and those who thought this could be better done if we had a vote within it.

It is not difficult to reconcile these results, since it may well have been appreciated that the freedom a country enjoys for independent action can be circumscribed as much by the intransigence of events as by the rules of an association it may join, and that self-determination is not necessarily accompanied by any more ability to safeguard one's own interest than might be offered by membership of a powerful group.

Two questions were asked in all three of our surveys, and it is of interest to examine the trends they display.

	1971 %	1974 %	1975 %
Britain, as an EEC member, has (will have) . . .			
more say in her own affairs	7	8	16
less say in her own affairs	74	63	46
equal, don't know	19	29	38
Britain can (will be able to) protect her interests better . . .			
in EEC	40	50	64
out of EEC	45	37	27
equal, don't know	15	13	9

In part, these trends may be due to experience of membership: it may not have been felt that much practical loss of autonomy had been observed since entry. But they probably also reflect growing awareness of worldwide problems, in the context of which Britain may seem very exposed and defenceless. Our findings on prices, given above, reflect this broader view. The most dramatic event which might have helped to give it wider currency was, perhaps, the sudden exercise of oil power by the Arabs late in 1973, but this was far from being the only reminder that Britain was no longer one of the world's most powerful nations.

The attractions of joining with others were therefore strong. Ninety-one per cent of those interviewed in 1974 agreed that 'Britain must unite with other countries to keep peace in the world', and 78 per cent that 'Britain's influence in the world depends on other countries' cooperation'. These views were probably less well-formed in 1971, but our survey in that year did not include questions which permit a close comparison. We do know, however, that 53 per cent of the electorate in 1971 already saw the need to link up with other countries, while 40 per cent did not.

The EEC was not, of course, the only possible partner. Another was the United States — an idea supported by 31 per cent in 1971. Yet another possibility was strengthening ties with the Commonwealth. There was certainly a widespread belief at that time that Commonwealth countries would suffer from Britain's entry into the EEC. Half the electorate thought this, but the view may well have been modified subsequently; at any rate, by 1975 only 10 per cent believed the Commonwealth countries wanted Britain to leave the EEC. A note of regret is struck by the 67 per cent who said in 1974 that 'Britain should have developed links with the Commonwealth rather than joined the Common Market', and by the 64 per cent who agreed that 'the Commonwealth nations are better friends to Britain than the French, Germans or anybody in Western Europe will ever be'. And a year later, in 1975, about nine out of ten electors wanted Britain to keep its links with the Commonwealth. A cautionary note may be added here: it seems from replies to subsidiary questions in 1971 that 'the Commonwealth' may have been thought of primarily in terms of the 'white Commonwealth' countries. When asked in 1974 whether, if Britain were to leave the EEC, she should join up with other countries, 59 per cent of the electorate said yes. Pressed for details, 36 per cent mentioned Australia, 34 per cent New Zealand, 27 per cent Canada. No other Commonwealth country was mentioned by more than 2 per cent, though 17 per cent named the USA.

One of the aims of links with other countries is to improve defence. On the whole, it was agreed in 1971 that this would be achieved by joining the EEC, and that view had strengthened by 1975, when very few indeed thought membership had any militarily weakening effect. It was not that the world was becoming more peaceful: doubts about the international situation generally may account for a less optimistic view being taken in 1974 than in 1971 about the contribution to world peace that Britain's EEC membership would make: 48 per cent thought it would make peace more secure, 42 per cent less secure, compared with 54 per cent and 31 per cent respectively in 1971.

Another of the themes of the debate was the extent to which the EEC should be a political or a purely economic union, and the 1974 survey investigated this. It might be expected that most opponents of membership, and a proportion of supporters, would be opposed to extending the Community's aims to political union, together resulting in a strong majority against. But this was not what was found. Instead, the electorate was fairly evenly divided. Forty-three per cent agreed, and 39 per cent disagreed, with the proposition that 'the Common Market countries should form a political union rather than only an economic union'. The remarkable lack of correlation between views about political union and general attitudes to the EEC can be shown by cross-analysis. If we divide the 1974 sample into three groups — anti, conditionally anti (i.e. anti unless better terms could be obtained), and pro (including conditionally pro), we can then examine the views of each group about political rather than only economic union.

	Anti %	Conditionally anti %	Pro %
Agreed (with political union)	41	46	40
No view expressed	23	22	14
Disagreed	36	32	46

It is in fact the supporters of EEC membership who seem to have the greatest reservations about political union, but differences between the three groups are not great. This is not as surprising as it may at first appear, since supporters of British membership of the EEC were primarily concerned about the economic benefits that would accrue to Britain.

In response to a further question, 47 per cent said they favoured 'the creation of a European government to handle European issues' — though the proportion shrank to 30 per cent when it was pointed out that in that event Britain, or any other country, would have to follow majority decisions it did not like. The difference between these last two responses may be due to pressure exerted by the second question (which arguably 'leads' people to give a different answer), but probably also reflects uncertainty resulting from the lack of definition of these notions, which have not, in this country at any rate, ever come to the forefront.

Another point which sometimes emerged during the debate was that EEC membership might benefit some sectors of the British population more than others. Certainly such views were held, but by no means universally. In 1971, 45 per cent agreed, and 35 per cent disagreed, that only the rich would benefit; and in 1974, 52 per cent agreed, and 35 per cent disagreed, that only businessmen would benefit. But few accepted the suggestion that Londoners would benefit particularly. The 1971 survey pushed this issue further by asking people which of a series of contrasted pairs would be more likely to benefit, and also by asking them to choose from a list the most and least likely beneficiaries. Entry was seen as helping the young rather than the old; it was also likely to favour management rather than workers, the skilled rather than the unskilled, industrialists rather than farmers, and businessmen rather than professional men. These results could indicate a feeling that the nature of the EEC was such as to favour the more prosperous, but they could equally well reflect a belief that any radical change is likely to benefit those who are most adaptable and best placed to meet its requirements. This would explain the almost universal expectation that young people will benefit more than old: young people do not necessarily possess economic strength *now*, but they are adaptable and energetic, and the future lies with them.

One of the most striking findings of the 1971 survey was the extent to which the public distinguished between the long and short term. In the short term, only 28 per cent expected advantages to accrue, compared with 86 per cent who expected disadvantages (notably increased prices). But opinion was divided about the long term: half foresaw advantages, half disadvantages. As a result, the view was widely held that in the long run our children would thank us for joining the EEC; and that view persisted. The 1974 figures are close to those for 1971 – and those for 1975 are more favourable to the EEC, perhaps partly because the question related to *staying* in rather than *getting* in but also because of the general swing to the EEC during that last year.

The campaign itself

It might be supposed that after such an extended debate on an issue

which must have seemed to many to be more a question of feeling than
of rational analysis, the public might have had more than enough of
Europe. This appears not to have been the case. About two thirds of
the sample in 1975 said they were either very or at least fairly interested in the campaign – a somewhat higher level of interest than they
admitted to taking in 'politics' generally, and than they had expressed
about the EEC a year earlier. It seems likely that the public had some
genuine feeling of involvement, though certainly not of urgent excitement, during the run-up to the referendum.

Levels of interest expressed by particular groups were fairly closely
related to turn-out (though the relationship is far from perfect), and we
find interest highest among groups noted in Chapter 5 as being most
inclined to vote: in particular, professional and managerial workers.
Unskilled or semi-skilled workers, and younger people, exhibited least
interest.

In spite of the apparent level of concern, only a small proportion
(3 per cent) attended any meetings on the subject, though this
proportion was larger among non-manual workers (7 per cent of the
professional and managerial group had attended at least one meeting).

The leaflets and the media

People were well aware of the three official leaflets circulated (one
setting out government policy, one the pro-market case and the other
the anti-market case). Eighty-nine per cent said they had received them,
6 per cent that they had not; 5 per cent that they did not remember.
Since they were sent to all households, it may be wondered why there
is any shortfall, but quite apart from any possibility of error in so large-
scale a delivery, it is known that written material can go astray for
other reasons (mislaid before being looked at, destroyed by a child or
family member other than the person interviewed, and so on). That so
high a proportion should positively recall the leaflets is therefore not to
be expected as an automatic consequence of wide distribution: it
indicates a fairly high level of interest as well as efficient means of
delivery.

Among those who did not vote in the referendum the proportion
recalling the leaflets fell to 79 per cent, 13 per cent saying they had not
received them. It is very unlikely that failure to vote was due to non-
receipt: the obvious explanation is that lack of interest – of which
non-voting is a consequence – led to the leaflets being disregarded or
forgotten.

Nevertheless, most of the non-voters *did* remember the leaflets and about 40 per cent of them claimed to have read them, compared with about 63 per cent of voters (the figures are almost, but not quite, identical for all three leaflets, each of which was the subject of separate questioning). Both those voting to stay in and those voting to leave paid equal attention to the leaflets; there was only the faintest trace of the tendency sometimes observed for more people to read, or at least to recall reading, the one that coincided with their view.

In view of their general orientation to the issue, it would not be surprising if non-manual workers were more likely to read the leaflets than manual workers were; in fact, this tendency is marginal, disappearing entirely in the case of the pro-market leaflet:

	Professional/ managerial	Other non-manual	Skilled manual	Semi/ unskilled
	%	%	%	%
% reading:				
Government leaflet	60	61	58	54
Pro-market leaflet	57	57	60	55
Anti-market leaflet	60	58	58	53

It is with age rather than socioeconomic group that claimed readership of the leaflets varies. This can be illustrated by figures for the government leaflet:

	% reading government leaflet
Aged under 30:	50
30-39	51
40-49	61
60 or over	67

But were the leaflets helpful? The evidence is conflicting. About a fifth of people who read them found them difficult to understand, and over a third claimed that the leaflets didn't give the sort of information they wanted. Still, one in six readers (10 per cent of the *total* sample) believed that the leaflets had helped them to make up their minds. The task of assessing the effect of mass communications of any kind is a remarkably difficult one, and we could not hope to do more in the compass of a few questions than to provoke a few thoughts about the effect of these leaflets. They seem not to have been a complete success, since they were thought by many to be insufficiently clear and informative. On the other hand, it may well be that the public sets standards that are too high: it wants information of a kind that cannot be provided. To this point we shall return later. It is probably unwise to expect too much from a single leaflet distribution; and if they really did help one voter in ten to make up his mind the leaflets may have done their job.

The leaflets were, of course, only one means of informing the public — and they were far less prominent in the campaign as a whole than were newspapers and television, according to a question which asked people from which source they had obtained most information about the EEC. Almost inevitably, television tops the list. As studies in other fields have shown, it often tends to be assumed that if something has been seen, it must have been on television (this has been demonstrated in relation to items which are known never to have appeared). The most interesting feature of the replies, tabulated below, is the extent to which friends and workmates were a prime source of information, implying that the issue was extensively discussed.

Found out most of information about EEC from:

Television	83%	Radio	17%
Newspapers	71%	Official leaflets	15%
Friends, relatives	23%	Workmates	12%

Other sources were also mentioned, but none individually by as much as 10 per cent.

The charge of bias was laid during the campaign at the door of some of the media, and we asked the public for its views on this. Most people did not think that coverage was biased, but a minority did. In the case of television, 8 per cent thought that the pro-market case was favoured, and 1 per cent the anti-market case. It will come as no surprise that these views are related to general attitudes to the issue and to voting behaviour. A rather larger proportion felt that there was bias among the press — 19 per cent in favour of the pro-market side and 1 per cent of the anti-market. Indeed, among those who voted to leave Europe, the proportion alleging pro-Europe bias rose to 33 per cent.

Getting the facts across

In spite of the barrage of information, only 44 per cent thought that the campaign had generally 'got over the facts' about the advantages and disadvantages of EEC membership, and only 37 per cent considered that the public had enough information to vote in a referendum. Those who voted to stay in were considerably more satisfied in this respect (49 per cent believing the campaign had got the facts across, compared with 37 per cent of those who voted to get out). At the personal level, 56 per cent believed that they themselves had enough information, and 40 per cent that they had not (4 per cent were not sure). When asked to say what else they would have liked, the 40 per cent mentioned an extremely varied range of topics which are difficult to summarise, and are sometimes of too general a nature to be very helpful. They included costs and benefits of membership; prices and living costs; agricultural and fishing policies; constitutional and administrative aspects; job opportunities and working conditions. Some of the replies pleaded for better quality of information rather than a greater quantity: they wanted it to be politically unbiased, and asked for 'the facts' (as opposed to subjective argument and opinion) in a simple presentation.

But what are the facts? One of the most fascinating aspects of the entire saga of Britain and the EEC is that a society which has been increasingly told of the scientific disciplines nowadays brought to bear on public decision-making finally learned that there was no way of predicting with any certainty what would happen either in Europe or out of it.

Levels of knowledge

How much, in fact, did the public know about the EEC or about the referendum? Because there are so few hard facts, this is difficult to assess, and most of our questions are either on peripheral matters, such as what view each political party held, or on points of detail such as the member countries comprising the EEC. People were mostly aware of the way the result of the referendum voting had gone in England. Although 10 per cent were not sure, virtually all the remaining 90 per cent replied correctly. Of those who had voted, 93 per cent knew the result. Separate analysis of England, Scotland and Wales shows that the residents of each were equally well informed about their own results; the English were rather less certain about the Scottish and Welsh results than were Scottish and Welsh residents about the outcome of the English voting.

Answers at the more local level were a little less assured. Seventeen per cent did not know the result for their county (or region, in

	English %	Scottish %	Welsh %
% giving correct result for:			
England	90	95	88
Scotland	72	87	78
Wales	73	71	87
Northern Ireland	70	73	68

Scotland). Nevertheless, the great majority were aware of it.

The stance of each of the political parties, and other countries, towards Europe was also pretty well understood. Here are the attributed views:

	Favour staying in %	Favour leaving %	Equally divided %	Not sure %
The government	80	1	15	4
Labour Party	49	15	31	5
Conservative Party	83	4	10	3
Liberal Party	68	6	7	19
Communist Party	7	61	*	32
Scottish Nat. Party	12	57	3	28
Welsh Nat. Party	16	38	4	42
Rest of Commonwealth	69	10	6	15
Rest of EEC	86	2	5	7

* = less than 0.5%

Looking separately at each party's stance as seen by its supporters instead of by the entire sample, we find that supporters of a party see it as being more pro-European than do non-supporters. This tendency is least marked with the Conservative Party, about whose position there was, perhaps, least doubt. Labour Party supporters tended a little to play down the extent to which their party was divided. Liberal Party supporters had a more clear-cut view of their party's policy, seeing it as more European than non-Liberals were inclined to suppose. The sample of SNP supporters interviewed was small (37); virtually all of them knew that the party's policy was to leave Europe. Among the still smaller sample of Plaid Cymru supporters (17) there was less unanimity about their party's position.

On the whole, men seemed better informed than women about the orientation of each party in relation to Europe. And levels of knowledge varied by occupational group, being highest among professional and managerial workers and lowest among the semi- or unskilled. Those voting to stay in showed themselves to know more about party stances than those voting to leave, and the latter in turn were better informed than those who did not vote.

A similar question was asked about the stance of ten leading politicians: did the respondent think each in turn was pleased or disappointed by the referendum result? The replies, as in the case of the parties, demonstrated a fairly high level of awareness:

| | Attributed attitude to referendum result: | | |
	Pleased %	Disappointed %	Don't know %
Benn	7	76	17
Castle	19	68	13
Foot	12	61	27
Powell	7	81	12
Shore	14	40	46
Callaghan	63	7	30
Heath	93	3	4
Thatcher	83	7	10
Thorpe	73	7	20
Wilson	91	3	6

It is interesting to see what variations occur between these names. The lowest levels of knowledge relate to Peter Shore, Michael Foot, Jim Callaghan and Barbara Castle, in that order. Most accurately stated are the views of the main party leaders, and of Enoch Powell. Not unexpectedly, the better known the politician, the better known were his views on the referendum result. Peter Shore, although a leading anti-EEC spokesman, was probably the least well-known politician in the list, and his prominence in the campaign was not enough to offset this.

An examination of the levels of knowledge of different population groups shows a pattern of variation similar to that commented on in relation to knowledge of party stances.

The last set of questions of this kind was based on knowledge of the member countries comprising the EEC, and has been a feature of each of SCPR's three surveys. Comparisons with earlier periods are thus possible, though there is a discontinuity between 1971 and 1974 because the EEC membership enlarged from six to nine countries. The proportion attributing membership to each country was as follows.

	1971 %	1974 %	1975 %
America	7	6	6
Belgium	72	80	85
Denmark	*	69	66
France	91	94	95
Holland	64	77	75
Italy	57	62	75
Luxemburg	43	54	59
Norway	17	28	16
Ireland	2	45	65
Russia	4	3	3
South Africa	4	3	2
Switzerland	21	19	16
United Kingdom	*	91	94
West Germany	77	78	85

* Denmark and the United Kingdom were not asked about in 1971.

It is convenient to consider the listed countries in three groups. First, those which have recently become members: the United Kingdom, Ireland and Denmark. All but a small proportion knew about the United Kingdom's membership, and about two thirds were aware that Denmark and Ireland are now members. Second, the original Six. Awareness of their status had steadily increased, though more sharply in some cases than others. There was still limited awareness of Luxemburg's membership; best known was France, followed by West Germany and Belgium, with Holland and Italy some way below. Belgium's comparatively high position on the list may owe something to the role of Brussels as the administrative centre of the EEC. Third, those that have never been members. Only Norway seems to have caused much confusion, particularly in 1974 when many people seem to have thought Norway's application to join had been carried through.

There was a general increase between 1974 and 1975 in the level of knowledge about countries comprising the EEC. This increase was on the whole pretty evenly spread between different population groups. There was some 'catching up' on the part of manual workers and a consequent reduction in, but not the disappearance of, the differences between the various socioeconomic groups. Non-voters did not catch up at all: starting from a lower baseline in 1974 their level of know-ledge of EEC countries increased no more than — perhaps less than — that of voters.

To complete this discussion of levels of knowledge, it is necessary to report what was said in reply to two questions in which people were asked to rate on a scale their own, and the public's, general levels of knowledge about the advantages and disadvantages of EEC member-ship.

	1971 %	1974 %	1975 %
Self:			
Very knowledgeable	1	3	3
Quite knowledgeable	23	29	39
Not very knowledgeable	54	54	47
Not at all knowledgeable	19	13	11
Public generally:			
Very knowledgeable	1	2	2
Quite knowledgeable	15	18	25
Not very knowledgeable	62	65	60
Not at all knowledgeable	19	11	9

Note: Residual categories (e.g. 'don't know') are omitted.

The rapid increase in knowledge in 1974-5, compared with the smaller changes between 1971 and 1974, is due to the campaign. But even the end-state, in 1975, shows the public taking a pretty sceptical view of its own state of knowledge; and this accords with our other findings. It is true that levels of knowledge in relation to political parties, politicians and EEC member countries were fairly high, but these are not what someone will feel he needs in order to take an intelligent decision on the issue. It is another kind of information — about the consequences of EEC membership or non-membership — that people felt they lacked, though they were not deterred by this from casting their votes.

Should there have been a referendum?

At the time of SCPR's 1971 survey the idea of a referendum had certainly been canvassed, but was not widely thought to be practical politics. As a result, it was given scant attention in the questionnaire, and was linked to the issue of information. As we have reported, most people did not consider themselves very knowledgeable. But did the public have *enough* information to vote in a referendum on this issue? No, said 84 per cent. Three years later, in 1974, after a great deal of further public debate and actual entry into the EEC, this percentage had shrunk, though only to 75 per cent. But the referendum campaign itself brought about a sharp additional reduction in 1975 to 37 per cent: a little ironically, this change was out of all proportion even to the claimed increase in individual respondents' knowledge about the issue, and still more to actual increases in levels of knowledge, insofar as these are indicated by the questions discussed earlier. But it may be that one of the lessons the public learned in the course of the campaign is that the decision did not really rest on knowledge anyway. Even experts did not seem too clear about just what difference membership had made. So the public may have come to set less store by knowledge about the issue, and as a result to feel more confident about participating in the decision.

The same trend is shown by another question asked in 1971 on the topic: did the respondent feel he himself had *enough* information? Eighteen per cent did in 1971 and in 1974; then in 1975 this proportion rose to 56 per cent.

There was one other question in 1971 which was concerned with the referendum issue. Did respondents think that it should be up to MPs to decide on entry? A similar question was included in 1974, though using a different technique, whereby respondents were asked to agree or disagree with the statement that 'it should be up to MPs to have the final say about whether Britain remains a member of the Common Market'.

The stability of the replies is striking, but both questions can be objected to on the grounds that they leave open whether the preferred alternative to Parliament is the *public* or the *government*. The former is

		1971 %	1974 %
Decision:	Up to MPs	38	39
	Not up to MPs	57	59
	No view expressed	5	2

the more natural interpretation, and is more consistent with the results of another question asked in 1974 (by which time the referendum had become a prominent issue), which showed a large majority (77 per cent) in favour of holding one. Among anti-marketeers this view was virtually unanimous, and even among pro-marketeers — who were less enthusiastic — it was supported by two out of every three.

But less than half the public, in 1974, thought it 'very likely' or 'fairly likely' that there would be a referendum. This might reflect the fact that the survey took place before the Labour Government's re-election in October of that year, but also suggests that the public was sceptical about, or ignorant of, the government's commitment to a referendum on the issue.

In 1975 the questioning on the referendum was extended still further. One of the things people were asked (after the event) was whether they had been in favour of the referendum or not. Interestingly, only 57 per cent now said they had favoured it, while 37 per cent said they had opposed it. This is a notable drop from the 77 per cent approving it in advance (in 1974), and suggests that the campaign may have led some people to doubt whether this kind of issue could after all be satisfactorily dealt with in that way. Nevertheless, it was still approved by a majority.

The pattern of changing views between June 1974 and June 1975 is best shown by analysing the replies given by the same people on two successive occasions:

51 per cent were *for* a referendum at both dates;
22 per cent were *for* it in 1974 but *against* it in 1975;
 5 per cent were *against* it in 1974 but *for* it in 1975;
12 per cent were *against* it at both dates.

The remaining 10 per cent did not express a definite view at the first date, or the second, or either.

There was a fairly even split over the desirability of future referenda on other issues: 45 per cent thought them desirable, while 50 per cent did not. The former were asked what sorts of issues would be suitable. The only single issue that figures prominently was capital punishment, which was suggested by about a third; references to it may merely reflect the fact that it has often been suggested as a possible referendum issue, and should not be taken to indicate it to be a considered priority on the part of the public. A wide variety of other topics was mentioned, including:

Prices	8%
Industrial relations/unions/strikes	7%
Laws on crime/punishment	6%
Wages	6%
Defence	5%

The appearance of prices in this list is probably due to widespread concern about them. But they do not seem suitable for treatment by referendum, and underline the point already made that the items cannot be taken as the public's considered suggestions.

People who favoured the EEC referendum also tend to favour referenda on other issues, and *vice versa*. But there are significant numbers of exceptions to this, as the following diagram illustrates, based on replies to the 1975 survey (see Figure 3).

Another way of presenting the same information is to divide the entire sample into four groups, as follows:

Favour both EEC and other referenda	37%
Favour EEC, not other	18%
Favour other, not EEC	7%
Favour neither	28%

The remaining 10 per cent did not express a view about one or other referendum, or about either.

Public views on the issue are seen to be rather fragmented. The fact that a substantial group favoured a referendum on the EEC issue alone may be a tribute to its unique constitutional importance, or may simply reflect the fact that the referendum became a political weapon in the EEC debate, during which it seemed that for some, at least, attitudes to the EEC were the principal cause of support for, or opposition to, a referendum. It would be silly to suggest that all referendum

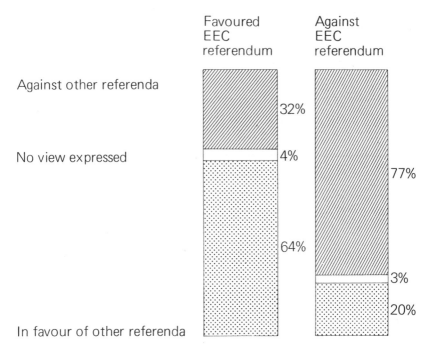

Figure 3

attitudes were dictated by the holder's attitude to the EEC, but it would be equally silly to believe that none were. The two issues became inextricably intertwined, and the analyst can only note the association between them without attributing any particular proportion of one to the influence of the other.

Whether referendum attitudes are independently formed or are derived from prior attitudes to the EEC, we find a good deal of consistency when we look at particular population groups. A group that is more in favour of the EEC referendum tends on the whole to favour other referenda also. The overall effect can be seen from Figure 4. For each group, a score has been calculated to summarise its attitude to the EEC referendum. This score is simply the difference between the proportion in favour and the proportion against. A similar score has been computed to summarise the group's attitude to other referenda. Figure 4 plots the two scores against each other — EEC on the x (horizontal) axis, others on the y (vertical) axis. The overall mean

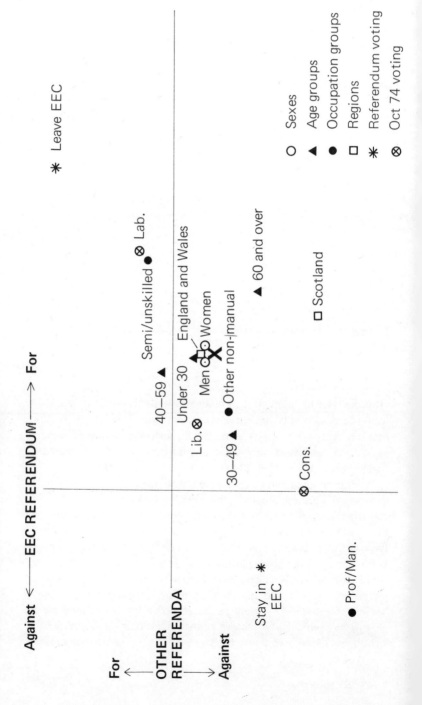

Figure 4. Comparison of attitudes to EEC and other referenda

position of the sample is indicated by a capital X. It will be seen that both the sexes are very close to this, and that the four age groups analysed are not far away. Scotland stands a little aside from England and Wales, being more in favour of the EEC referendum but less favourable to others. There is a marked difference between socio-economic groups, however: professional and managerial workers are opposed to all referenda, and there is a progression through other non-manual and skilled manual workers to the semi- or unskilled, who tend to be in favour of both the EEC referendum and others. This pattern is echoed by the disposition of the political parties — Conservatives opposed, Labour in favour and Liberals intermediate. Finally, we may note from the diagram that those in favour of EEC membership tend to be anti-referendum, those against it pro-referendum.

In conclusion

The public responded positively to the referendum. They believed the EEC issue to be an important one, and a good deal of interest was aroused. People talked about it among themselves, and noted the information provided. They wanted more facts and fewer opinions from the government and the media; they were diffident about their own knowledge, but they felt able to form a strongly held view and cast a vote, realising perhaps that even the experts did not really know the answers.

Although opinion swung from anti to pro during the period covered by our surveys, the issues remained the same throughout. At the end as at the beginning, EEC membership seemed to be a long-run benefit for which our children would thank us. Yes, we did have to sacrifice autonomy — but what *is* autonomy in the modern, interdependent world? We would be able to look after ourselves better, both economically and militarily, if we were in a powerful group. Yes, it may put prices up even faster. But then perhaps it will help wages to rise, too. 'Anyway', one of our respondents said, 'it was the only thing, wasn't it? If we didn't go in, we'd be finished.' Once we were in, the absence of adverse consequences that could be positively attributed to membership combined with conservatism to encourage the public to vote for keeping the new *status quo* rather than facing a fresh upheaval. There were regretful glances back towards the Commonwealth, with which most people felt links should be maintained, but even if they were not everyone's first choice as partners, the EEC countries were sufficiently acceptable to provide Britain with the reinforcement the public felt she needed.

References

1. *Britain and the EEC*, Barry Hedges and Roger Jowell, SCPR.
2. *The Grudging Europeans*, Roger Jowell and James Spence, SCPR, March 1975 (fieldwork conducted in 1974).
3. *Methodological report on the 1975 referendum survey*, Barry Hedges, SCPR, November 1975.
4. Uwe Kitzinger, *Diplomacy and Persuasion*, Thames and Hudson (1973), p. 360.

4 THE MEDIA AND THE MESSAGES
Dipak Nandy

As we turn to the last weeks of the referendum campaign, it becomes
more and more relevant to ask: How effective were the mass media in
informing the public and assisting it to reach a decision? How successful were they in responding to the novel features of the occasion? Did
they do justice, not only to the parties in the argument, but to the
issues facing the nation? In this chapter we look at some of the evidence
and attempt to reach an interim verdict.

It may be useful to rehearse three background factors against which
the media's response to the campaign should be assessed. First, for the
best part of a decade — from the decision of the Wilson Cabinet to
apply for entry in May 1967 to the end of February 1975, when the
decision to hold a referendum was announced — the inability of governments of either party to sponsor 'The Great Debate' on the issues
involved in Britain's membership of the EEC constituted what might
be called 'the grumbling complaint' of British politics. In the Cabinet
discussions of April-May 1967, according to Mr Wilson, the fullest
possible information was made available to every Minister involved:
'If anyone had asked for a document on the effect of entry into the
Market on British pigeon fancying, he would have got it';[1] the electorate, however, had to be content with a succession of White Papers, the
most notable of which is memorable chiefly for its estimate that the
cost of British entry might be as low as £100m. or as high as £1,100m.,[2]
a conclusion justly described by Mr Wilson as 'somewhat negative'.

Mr Heath's administration, having promised that entry would be
effected only with 'the full-hearted consent' of the British people,
proceeded to treat its parliamentary majority as an adequate substitute
for popular consent. Throughout this period, as we have seen in earlier
chapters, the electorate was strikingly aware of its lack of knowledge of
the issues involved. It is not unfair to say that in June 1971 it was
treated to a Fanfare for a Europe about which it knew little. Neither
party, when in office, had exerted itself unduly to provide the information or to promote the debate that had been promised and that the
magnitude of the decision clearly demanded.

The situation, therefore, was tailor-made for the media of mass
communications, yet it has to be recorded that the media did not

contribute in any substantial sense to the promotion of an informed discussion of the question between 1967 and 1975. The BBC's one mammoth attempt to promote 'The Great Debate' in the spring of 1971 was summarily if unforgettably dismissed by its own presenter, Mr Robin Day, as 'the great cockup'. There was, in short, a felt absence of information and debate, and the mass media did nothing to fill the void left by the major political parties.

A second important background factor, of direct relevance to the media's treatment of the referendum, is the fact that it had been preceded by two general elections in the previous year. The October election had confirmed the Tory debacle of February without producing a clear Labour majority in Parliament. It had also confirmed the conviction of the mass media (and particularly of broadcasters) that the nation was war-weary. There was a pervasive sense – easy to recall, difficult to document – that parties and politicians had been overexposed. However Millite radicals may lament it, there was an understandable feeling among broadcasters and journalists that enough was enough, and a temptation – again understandable, though it should have been more strongly resisted – to regard the referendum of June 1975 as the third general election in eighteen months. In short, the line of least resistance for the mass media was to cast the referendum into the more familiar general election mould. Once that had been done, the mood of battle fatigue that we have described virtually dictated low-key rather than high-key treatment, less rather than more coverage, of the issues.

The third background factor was the spectacular emergence of inflation as the dominant issue in politics by the autumn of 1974. By itself, inflation might have been the strongest card for the anti-marketeers to play. But the Yom Kippur war of 1973, and the quadrupling of oil prices in the ensuing twelve months, had manifestly nothing to do with the EEC. The magnitude of the inflationary effect of the oil price rise was visible for all to see, and effectively dwarfed the claim that Britain's inflationary problem was peculiarly connected with membership of the EEC. (Edward Heath's reiterated claim, in the two election campaigns of 1974, that price rises in Britain were the consequence of international processes outside Britain's control, finally carried conviction with the public.) At one stroke, the anti-marketeers were deprived of a substantial argument, while the pro-marketeers gained, through the winter of 1974-5, with all the publicity about the need to save energy, a dramatic, easily visualised metaphor to sum up their case: the world was a cold place where Britain had to huddle together with such friends as she could find for a little warmth. The implication of this potent metaphor scarcely needed to be made explicit. The unspoken implication, 'this is no time to go it alone', hung over the entire campaign and arguably determined its outcome.

Reporting and exploring the issues

In their treatment of the campaign there were significant variations in the performances of individual newspapers, individual programmes, different programme companies. The 'heavy' newspapers — *The Times*, the *Guardian*, the *Daily Telegraph*, the *Financial Times* — were judged, by both Britain in Europe, the pro-market lobby, and the National Referendum campaign, the anti-market lobby, not only to have been fair to the two camps, but also to have dealt with the issues in depth.

The *Guardian*, to take just one example, carried a series of full page 'Europe Extra' articles devoted to specific issues. The issue of 8 May 1975 was devoted to the EEC's trade patterns, its foreign aid record, and the implications of the Common Agricultural Policy for the Third World. Here, against a background of focused fact, balance of argument was as relevant as it was necessary. On the same page on which Harold Jackson and Rosemary Collins described the facts about aid, trade and the CAP, Judith Hart and Uwe Kitzinger presented opposing points of view on what EEC membership meant for Britain's own trading patterns, her ability to provide foreign aid to Third World countries, and so on.

But the combined circulation of these exemplary newspapers was still dwarfed by the mass appeal papers: the *Mirror*, the *Sun*, the *Daily Express*. For these papers, the main interest of the referendum campaign centered on the split within the Labour Party and the personality of Tony Benn: traditional angles with a traditional appeal. 'Row inside Labour Party', and 'Benn attacks . . .' were the stereotype headlines as the campaign unfolded, with 'Healey attacks Benn' as the chief variation. In the last week of the campaign, Edward du Cann attempted to wheel out a Tory anti-market bandwagon, but this vehicle, despite excited attention from the *Express* and the *Mail*, proved not to be roadworthy. Taken as a whole, it was the general election, second replay, as far as the popular dailies were concerned.

Newspapers are not, however, the chief source of information for the public, nor are they the most credible source of information. A study by the Centre for Mass Communications Research of Leicester University showed that 50 per cent of respondents regarded television as their main source of news, while 28 per cent regarded newspapers as their main source. If there were conflicting accounts of the same story in both media, 66 per cent said they trusted television more, as opposed to 18 per cent who placed greater reliance on newspapers.[3] (Public response remained true to this pattern in the referendum campaign, as we have seen in Chapter 3.)

The coverage of the referendum campaign on radio and TV differed from press coverage in one important aspect. As at any general election, radio and TV were under an obligation to provide to the contestants an agreed number of broadcasts, corresponding to the party political broadcasts. An arrangement was agreed at a special meeting at 10 Downing Street on 24 April 1975 of the main political parties, Britain in Europe, the National Referendum Campaign, the BBC and the IBA. The arrangement treated BIE and the NRC effectively as the parties at a general election, and allocated broadcasting time as follows:

Television: For each of the two organisations: four broadcasts of ten minutes.
Radio: For each of the two organisations: three broadcasts of ten minutes, two of five minutes.

'News reporting of the campaign will continue until polling day when referendum news will be restricted to matters arising directly from the progress of the poll. There will be no political broadcasts or comment on the European issue on the eve of polling day.'[4] This element of the broadcasters' output follows the conventional pattern of party political agreements. The special problems of dealing with a referendum, in which all parties, from left to right, were split, arose with the remainder of the broadcasting coverage — in the day-to-day news and current affairs output. The Director-General of the BBC, Sir Charles Curran, put his finger on the special problem posed for both the BBC and the IBA when he replied to a questioner that the BBC's aim in a referendum campaign

'has to be exactly the same as in any other political situation — to achieve fairness. The only trouble is that we've had our standard guideline removed. The reflection approximately of the balance in Parliament is no longer there because the decision has been committed to the country and there is a yes-or-no question. I think, therefore, that we are bound to settle to some sort of 50-50 division of time and opportunity.'[5]

There is clearly a wrestle here between the old formula and the new event. There is a recognition that much that is to come can only uneasily (and sometimes only dishonestly) be fitted into the mechanistic framework of the 50:50 formula. 'News', said Sir Charles, 'doesn't happen in a balanced way. You therefore report it when it comes.'[6] The Chairman of the Board of Governors was even more explicit:

'On the question of a 50:50 balance, there are, however, areas where forcing things into an artificial balance of this sort would be meaningless, or even dishonest . . . Things will go on happening, and we shall go on reporting them in our news bulletins. And if on some days, or even some weeks, the news falls out such that one side or the other in the campaign gets more prominence, we shall not seek to manipulate it in the interests of balance.'[7]

What is involved here is an essentially passive conception of the role of broadcasting. It assumes the existence of a plethora of interest groups, clamouring for airtime for their respective points of view. The role of the broadcasting organisation is reduced almost to that of the 'nightwatchman' state of classical liberalism — holding the ring for the contestants. The central preoccupation is with the multiplicity of ways in which the application of the 50:50 formula might be endangered by the awkward facts of political life. It reflects an essentially defensive posture: the concern is not with innovative broadcasting, but with ensuring that there are no possible grounds for criticism.

The nature and quality of the broadcasting output was varied. BBC Radio, for example, started its campaign coverage earlier, carried regular items of referendum news on, for example, *Newsbeat* on Radio 1, along with more extended treatment of issues on Radio 4, while using *Referendum Call*, a phone-in programme, to keep track of issues as the public saw them. There was an attempt, in other words, not only to spot stories, but to stay with them. (The contribution of commercial radio was, for all practical purposes, negligible.) On the other hand, unlike BBC Radio, television as a whole did not seriously begin its major efforts until the last three weeks. The programme companies as much as the BBC seemed to feel the tug of conservatism and routine, to see the referendum as a general election and to treat it, wearily, as such.

But there was a difference. The effort to do justice to a special event was much more readily apparent on ITV than it was on BBC Television. Anglia TV was the first off the mark with a series of three programmes designed to get at the nature of the creature, the European Common

Market. The first programme filmed two pro-market MPs at Brussels and Strasbourg, and back in their constituencies answering questions (4 April); the second programme repeated the exercise with two anti-market MPs (11 April); in the final programme, two of the four MPs were invited into a studio discussion, with viewers invited to phone in live with questions (18 April). Balance was thus scrupulously observed, but for the sake of answering viewers' questions about the Common Market, not for the sake of maintaining a balance.

Granada's first 90-minute programme on 19 May used the 'fly-on-the-wall' technique to look 'Inside the EEC' and to *show* (rather than to tell) viewers what happened. London Weekend's special 90-minute *Weekend World* programme on 1 June was deliberately constructed to explore issues rather than to provide a 'balanced' platform for the views of the accredited partisans.

The BBC's output on television was of the more familiar kind. *Nationwide*, on BBC 1, carried interviews with Geoffrey Rippon, Barbara Castle, Neil Marten and the Prime Minister, while *Newsday*, on BBC 2, interviewed Roy Hattersley, Sir Geoffrey Howe, Eric Heffer, Edward Taylor and Margaret Thatcher. *Talk-In*, on BBC 1, had Harold Wilson and Margaret Thatcher in the studio answering viewers' questions. The high points of the BBC's coverage were the set-piece confrontations, first between Powell and Shirley Williams and then between Roy Jenkins and Tony Benn; then *Midweek*'s 'At the Market' (three programmes); and, of course, the televising of the Oxford Union Debate, 'A Question of Europe', on 3 June. It was not the most imaginative example of the BBC's approach to programme making.

The 75-minute Oxford Union debate was compulsive viewing, but in fact the BBC simply 'reported' an on-going event. Granada's two-hour-long 'The Great Debate' the previous night was specially planned to exhibit all the nuances of argument involved. The first was 'televising' an event; the second was using television to illuminate an argument. In any event, ITV's 'Bus round the Market' attracted larger audiences (according to both JICTAR and BBC Audience Research figures) than 'The Great Debate', and very likely did more to inform viewers of the human reality of the EEC than either of the two set-piece debates.

Judgements about the adequacy and depth of coverage of an event such as the referendum campaign will inevitably have an element of subjective assessment about them. Judgements about the extent of coverage are less likely to be subjective, although measurement of column inches introduces a quite spurious air of precision into such judgements. Nor are audience measurements of very great assistance:

quite apart from the consistent contradiction between the BBC's
figures and JICTAR's, there is the difficulty of knowing what conclusions, in the present context, flow from *any* set of viewing figures.
For example, the BBC's Audience Research figures show the following
viewing figures for *Nationwide*'s interviews with four leading politicians:

29 May 1975	Geoffrey Rippon	24.2% of viewing audience
30 May	Barbara Castle	16.2%
2 June	Neil Marten	17.1%
3 June	Harold Wilson	14.2%

The reader is invited to draw his own conclusion from these figures.
The *post facto* assessment of Bernard Davies, interesting because he
approved of the BBC's low-key approach, was that: 'On this occasion
it was ITV which mounted the exhaustive campaign, whilst the BBC
showed some sense of proportion by limiting the hours spent in coverage.'[8]
    The rationale of the BBC's limited, traditional and low-key coverage,
with its far greater emphasis on maintaining fair balance, was in our
view two-fold. First, there is the general background reason that those
with a complaint or grievance about bias are more likely to direct it at
the BBC than at commercial TV. Because everyone owning a set pays
(or is supposed to pay) a license fee, the BBC generates a quite special
proprietary feeling. 'Irate viewer' does not feel quite the same sense of
outraged ownership when Granada or Thames is involved as he does
about the BBC. To this general expectation of the BBC by the viewing
public must be added the specific attacks on the coverage of the campaign by the BBC (and the BBC alone) which surfaced spectacularly
with Tony Benn's May Day rally speech: 'The BBC motto', he is
reported as saying, 'is "Nation shall speak peace unto nation". But
today, in many of its programmes on current affairs on radio and
television, the BBC seems to be fast becoming the mouthpiece of a
cynical and defeatist section of the middle class, scarcely bothering to
conceal its contempt for working people, their problems, their aspira-
tions and their views' (*Daily Mail*, 5 May). The response of the
Director-General to this quite egregiously unsustainable proposition
was to re-emphasise that assiduous column inch counting was under
way at the BBC: 'The fact of the matter is that we are keeping a
scrupulous watch on all our news and current affairs broadcasts', he is
quoted as saying in reply (*Daily Mail*, 5 May). Such an emphasis could
scarcely have been conducive to adventurous attempts to ensure a more

comprehensive coverage of issues or their more original presentation.

In any event, another reason for the BBC's low-key coverage was its own findings of audience reaction to the coverage of the general elections of the previous year. This revealed that the extended 9.00 p.m. *News* and *Election 74* (in February) drew smaller audiences than the shorter 8.50 p.m. *News* in 1970. The result was a decision to trim the BBC's coverage of the autumn general election campaign, a decision that was thought to be justified by the widespread complaints of boredom with politics. What was involved for the BBC programme planners in the spring of 1975, then, was a judgement about the kind of event the referendum was supposed to be. Influenced undoubtedly by the findings of its Audience Research Department, the BBC chose to regard the referendum, not as an unprecedented event on which the electorate wanted more information and informed discussion than it received, but merely as a third general election. The result of such a decision was almost certainly to inhibit the BBC's willingness to explore novel ways of examining and presenting the issues. Balance was achieved, but at the cost of doing adequate justice to the novelty of the occasion.

An obsessive desire for balance

What can fairly be said of the media (though with differing force in relation to different parts of the media) is that they overreacted to accusations of bias by being excessively cautious in the treatments of issues and events, and excessively, even obsessively, concerned with arithmetical balance. Papers with pugnacious editors, such as the *Sunday Times*, could shrug off charges of bias. It had been so consistently pro-market, anyway, that no one felt particularly outraged by its continuing pro-market stance, although no one complained either, as far as we know, of lack of coverage given to the anti-market campaign. On the other hand, a national institution like the BBC was, as its Director-General complained, 'on a hiding to nothing whatever we do in the Referendum campaign' (*Daily Mail*, 5 May). Specially sensitive to charges of bias, anxious about losing more viewers to ITV, it retreated into a low-profile, play-safe style of coverage. What was affected was the in-depth treatment of the issues.

There can be no serious dispute that the anti-marketeers elevated the issue of 'balance' virtually into a campaign issue in itself. Whether this was deliberate strategy is immaterial, for the net result was to make the mass media exceptionally sensitive to the question of balance. The anti-marketeers began, right from the start, before the NRC came into

existence, with a declared conviction that the mass media were suspect
and had to prove their fairness by providing balanced treatment of the
pro- and anti- campaigns. As early as November 1974, Christopher
Frere-Smith was claiming that 'not only rich individuals were on the
side of the Community, but also nearly every other national newspaper,
the BBC and the media' (*The Times*, 26 November). Peter Shore
weighed in the following month with an attack on 'the editor and
chief contributor of *The Times* and the great majority of those who
control and have controlled the current affairs programmes of the
BBC for the past decade for whom membership of the EEC has long
been a quasi-religious cult', and added, for good measure, that 'though
few in number, the unconditional marketeers have a formidable influence in the press and other media' (*The Times*, 14 December). Lord
Wigg went even further when he claimed that 'the media, committed to
EEC membership, are determined at all costs to prevent the people
from learning the truth' (*The Times*, 10 January 1975). At the
launching of the National Referendum Campaign, Mr Neil Marten had
stressed that 'the Press, TV and radio would have to give a fair presentation of the issues' (*Financial Times*, 8 January). Two months later,
at the beginning of the campaign proper, this was still his principal
concern: 'Mr Marten's chief preoccupation', wrote Robert Chesshyre,
'is with fair play: he has been to see the chairmen of the IBA and
BBC and said – with a meaningful look – that the campaign would be
monitoring press coverage and measuring column inches. "It will be a
classic study of press fairness", he said' (*Observer*, 16 March).

(It is a widespread misconception that the BBC is obliged by its
Charter to observe 'balance' or 'impartiality'. These words do not
appear in any of the BBC's Charters, past or present. They are to be
found in a letter of Lord Normanbrook, then Chairman of the Board
of Governors, to the Postmaster General, dated 19 June 1964. These
duties and their interpretation and application are entirely self-imposed
responsibilities. All that the BBC acknowledges is a duty to observe
'due impartiality' in the treatment of controversial subjects, a very
different matter from 'balance' *per se*, though the error is perhaps
understandable given the widespread confusion in contemporary
English usage between 'objective', 'balanced', 'impartial' and 'neutral',
words commonly used interchangeably.)

The outcome of the NRC's attacks on the media was of dubious
value to them, for, as a criterion in assessing media performance, the
concept of 'balance' has one major disadvantage. 'Balanced' treatment
of a controversial issue does not in itself guarantee that the issue has

been adequately explored. The coverage given to an argument, its style of presentation, may be 'balanced', but we cannot deduce from this that all the points of view on the question will have been adequately represented or, indeed, that justice will have been done to the issues involved. Given their provenance in small and frequently outcast groups in their respective parts of the political spectrum, it was a strange error for the NRC strategists to make, for it has been the traditional complaint of minority parties in British politics that 'balance', formally defined, counted in column inches or in number of programme hours allocated, tends to exclude points of view that happen to lie outside the 'consensus' of the day. But what is clear is that if the media were obsessed with balance, that obsession was largely forced upon them by the anti-marketeers. The natural response of the media, if the requirements of 'balanced' treatment and, say, 'comprehensive' or 'adequate' treatment came into conflict, would in these circumstances have been to opt for 'balance'. It would have required a strong editorial intervention to do otherwise.

If we attempt to judge the performance of the mass media by the standards they set themselves — balanced treatment of the opposing points of view and fairness of presentation — the conclusion must be that the media adhered scrupulously to the rule book. It would be hard to find adherents of either side in the campaign who would dissent from that conclusion.

Yet that cannot be the sole criterion of judgement. As British Rail and the railway unions remind us every year, too close an adherence to the rule book can effectively guarantee that trains never get to their destinations on time, perhaps never get there at all. At least as important as considerations of balance and fairness is the consideration of adequacy of treatment. The two requirements do not necessarily coincide, and when they come into conflict, the Fourth Estate of the realm is in a peculiarly exposed position, thrown back upon its own strength of nerve and on not much else if it elects to go for in-the-round and in-depth treatment of issues as its first priority.

Campaign strategies

Britain in Europe (BIE) must have been substantially influenced at its formative stage by an early assessment of the personalities on either side of the debate which showed clearly a heavy positive rating of the leading pro-marketeers (Jenkins, Shirley Williams, Heath, Whitelaw, Thorpe and Steele) and a startlingly negative rating of the leading anti-marketeers and those associated in the public mind with the

anti-European case: an unpopularity poll in which the Reverend Ian
Paisley led by lengths, followed by Powell and Benn at a fairly equal
distance, with Shore not far behind. To the extent, then, that the
mass media concentrated on personalities, BIE could afford to relax: a
campaign dominated by 'image' would suit them very well indeed. But
it would be neither fair nor accurate to imply that the BIE campaign
was 'image'-dominated: after all, politicians like Roy Jenkins, Edward
Heath and Shirley Williams who were, in the words of a prominent
pro-European, 'prepared to go for bust' on the issue of Britain's membership were hardly likely to pass up the opportunity to argue the
merits of their case.

It was, in fact, the National Referendum Campaign (NRC) that
focused the attention of the media on personalities, since one common
element among the leading anti-market figures — whether on the far
right, like Enoch Powell, or on the left and moving in a sinister trajec-
tory, like Tony Benn — was a grudging and long-standing dislike of the
press and of broadcasting. Indeed, both Powell and Benn had, at
different stages in their careers, extracted mileage from carefully
considered outbursts against the bias of the mass media. So on this
issue as well, the anti-marketeers to a very large extent created their
own scourge. Clive Irving once observed that the mass media always
tend to overreact to attacks on their integrity from figures like Agnew
and Powell, and to overcompensate by giving undeserved attention to
whoever accuses them, however preposterously, of political bias and
suppression. And that is precisely what happened in the referendum.

A second factor relevant to the content of the campaigns had to do
with the particular chemistry between a set of issues and the mood of
a society at a given point in time: the strategy of the anti-marketeers
centred on the major issues of prices, unemployment and the loss of
sovereignty. In any general election these would have been very powerful cards indeed, and NRC held them. The problem facing the pro-
marketeers, in fact, was how they could avoid confining the argument
to the narrow question of whether prices had risen because of EEC
membership or not, so as to broaden the narrow front of the prices
argument into a much wider engagement on the issue of Britain's food
supply. Quite apart from its intrinsic importance as an issue, it drew
the eye, so to speak, to BIE's conception of the central question
before the electorate: Britain *in* Europe or Britain alone?

But the prices issue was clearly one that the NRC wanted to exploit.
Indeed, one of the major questions to be answered about the referendum campaign as a whole may well be why, holding such a hand, the

anti-marketeers came to lose as decisively as they did. The answer may be that the mass media *did* get one message across: it was in effect an SOS from a nation in crisis to itself. No one in the autumn of 1974 or the spring of 1975 doubted that Britain was in the midst of an exceptionally severe economic crisis, or that the referendum decision was, in some ill-defined way, critically relevant to our ability to cope with the crisis. Against that background, it can now be seen that the campaign strategy of the anti-marketeers contained the seeds of its own destruction. The more the anti-marketeers emphasised the issue of unemployment, the more Tony Benn sought and attracted attention with his claims that membership of the EEC had cost Britain half a million or 700,000 jobs, the more frightened the electorate became. (By the end of May, according to a private opinion poll conducted on behalf of the Referendum Steering Group, 46 per cent agreed with the proposition that unemployment was bound to rise if Britain left the EEC.) The NRC campaign was seen by its opponents as delivering more and more 'Yes' votes the more it dwelt upon what BIE had diagnosed as the fear of loneliness in a cold world. 'It was important, we felt', one leading pro-marketeer put it, 'to keep Benn talking.'

There may be an element of cynicism in such a view, but the situation was one of the anti-marketeers' own construction. After all, the fracas, if one of Tony Benn's pronouncements had *not* been given prominent treatment, would have assumed unprecedented dimensions. If Benn chose to talk, the NRC had, by its own consistent accusations of bias in the media, guaranteed banner headlines for whatever Benn said. If Benn chose to talk doom, the media dutifully reported it.

The outcome, however, was quite clearly the opposite of that intended either by the NRC or by Tony Benn. It was to dramatise and make more precise the 'cold world' metaphor. The outcome is most accurately caught in a Franklin cartoon, reproduced here, which appeared in the *Sun* (2 June). A leading anti-marketeer observed plaintively afterwards, about the 'life raft syndrome' as he called it: 'One rather felt that if we had come up with a comparable alternative, then it would have been a different proposition.' What the NRC ran short of, however, was not the dramatic metaphor, but, quite simply, credibility. Faced with the threat of doom to come, the electorate looked for safe company, and it chose what seemed to be the more reliable crew to steer it into safer waters.

The initial strategy of the NRC was to underline the sheer diversity of the anti-market coalition as one of its main strengths: it was a strategy of contradiction publicly embraced. As a leading anti-marketeer

This cartoon was first published 2 June 1975 and is reproduced by kind permission of the *Sun* newspaper and the Artist.

put it: 'the aim was to show that *dis*unity is strength, to emphasise our differences, thereby emphasising the extraordinary weight of our case.' But this element of the strategy did not always work, as on the notorious occasion, during Granada's 'The Great Debate', when Tony Benn refused to sit next to Enoch Powell. As the campaign developed, therefore, the NRC's very strengths began to turn one by one into liabilities. The heterogeneity in which they had placed so much hope at the start of 1975 came to be seen more and more as an implausible collection of eccentrics driven into a temporary alliance. The *Observer* (16 March) had diagnosed in March that the 'anti-marketeers have to be careful about their bed-fellows . . . Inevitably, they attract some eccentric support. There is a Hampshire woman who flies a black-edged Union Jack at half-mast on the anniversary of EEC entry.' So the NRC's strategy of emphasising that 'disunity is strength' backfired. The conception was bold. Whether it was wise is another matter. Effective it certainly was not. But for this the mass media cannot be held responsible.

Students of mass communications have commented on the way in which the mass media seem predisposed to cast events into a number of small, ready-to-hand, stereotyped categories.[9] An unprecedented event, such as a referendum, therefore challenges the responsiveness and in-genuity of broadcasters and journalists. Their temptation was to play safe, to force the new, the unconventional, the unprecedented event into a familiar and manageable stereotype. 'As the campaign developed', Mr Christopher Frere-Smith observed, 'it developed far too much like a general election. We had to emphasise that this was not a general election, that they were not voting for or against a government, that they were not being disloyal to a party. We failed to stress the differ-ence [between a referendum and a general election]. It was not on the issues that the people voted.' If that is true, it would be in our view, quite wrong to convict the mass media alone of default. The message of the media, in so far as there was such a thing, was that Britain was in a crisis, that there were two teams of people proposing rival courses and that the media were trying hard to present their views fairly. They cannot, therefore, be held responsible for the electorate's decision that the pro-marketeers seemed to field a more plausible team, which had the added advantage of having the incumbent administration on its side, while a coalition composed of Benn, Powell and Shore, with Foot in attendance on one side and Paisley on the other, was good for nothing beyond an anti-market campaign.

Our conclusion then is that there *was*, in the spring of 1975, a public demand for information about the issues; that the mass media did have a rare opportunity to promote informed democratic debate; that the response of different sections of the media varied considerably, but that the attempts by Anglia, Granada, Thames and LWT certainly showed that there was no inherent 'bias against understanding' in television; that substantially the news media ended up by treating the referendum as an extra general election (sometimes, as with the BBC, for the wrong reasons), but that this was largely the result, not of the broadcasters' failure of imagination, but of the anti-marketeers' fierce and consistent pressure for 'balance' – a pressure that forced journalists and broadcasters into the familiar and practised style of presentation of election campaigns, as though they were dealing with an awkward, mutant general election rather than a referendum. An opportunity was missed. But it would be wrong to think that the main responsibility for the missed opportunity can be placed at the door of the mass media.

References

1. Harold Wilson, *The Labour Government 1964-70* (1971), p. 387.
2. *Britain and the European Communities: An Economic Assessment*, HMSO, Cmnd. 4289, February 1970.
3. P. Croll, *The Future of Broadcasting: a preliminary report*, mimeograph from Centre for Mass Communications, Leicester University, February 1973.
4. *BBC Record*, No. 96, May 1975, pp. 3-4.
5. Press Conference, 24 April 1975, in *BBC Record*, No. 96, p. 2.
6. *BBC Record*, No. 96, p. 2.
7. *BBC Record*, No. 94, March 1975, p. 3.
8. *Broadcast*, 16 June 1975.
9. Johan Galtung and J. D. Halloran among others: see *Demonstrations and Communication*, Halloran *et al.* (1970), p. 26.

5 WHO VOTED WHAT
Martin Collins

Two out of three eligible people turned out to vote in the EEC referendum. And two out of three votes cast were in favour of staying in the Common Market on the renegotiated terms. The turnout, lower than in a general election, may have disappointed some, but the government could draw satisfaction from the size of the 'Yes' majority and from the fact that only two areas — the Scottish island authorities of the Western Isles and Shetland — returned majorities against Britain's continued membership.

Before the referendum, it was feared that the result might be divisive rather the decisive — that some parts of the United Kingdom might vote clearly to stay in while others voted equally clearly to get out. The possibility of such division was a source of controversy in the design of the referendum. The government's original plan was for a central count of the votes that would produce an overall verdict with no indications of any regional differences of opinion. But there were calls, especially from anti-market groups, for a count on the conventional basis of parliamentary constituencies.

The eventual design was a compromise. Instead of the 600-plus constituency returns at a general election, only sixty-eight returns were made at the referendum. Fifty-four were from the counties of England and Wales, plus one from the Isles of Scilly; twelve were from the Scottish regions, including one each from Orkney and Shetland, and one was from the province of Northern Ireland.

The sixty-eight returning areas ranged widely in size, from the 1,500 electors of the Isles of Scilly to the five million plus of Greater London. Since the overall verdict was reached by aggregating the votes nationally, this variation did not introduce inequity. It has, however, limited our ability to use the returns as a basis for understanding the voting pattern. Generally, the large size and heterogeneity of the returning areas smoothed out the differences between them. The few returns for extremely small areas may stand out from the general pattern simply because of their smallness.

The smoothing effect of the returning system can be seen from the results of the October 1974 general election, taken county by county. Of the forty-six English counties, only seven produced an overall

majority for one party, and in half of them no single party received as
many as 45 per cent of the votes cast. This pattern is in marked contrast to the pattern of constituency returns. Of the 500-plus English
constituencies, over 200 produced an overall majority for one candidate,
and in fewer than a quarter of them did no one candidate receive 45
per cent of the votes.

How much of the apparent uniformity of the referendum results
was a direct result of the way the votes were counted? Would a more
detailed breakdown of the votes have caused the government some
embarrassment, with several constituencies voting 'No'? Or would it
have produced an even more convincing demonstration of a general
wish to remain in the EEC?

In the analysis that follows, we consider this and other wider
questions. We seek to identify groups of people, distinguishable by their
political sympathies or their demographic characteristics, who seem to
have been particularly inclined to vote 'Yes', to vote 'No', or to abstain.
This is done by relating the referendum results to the characteristics of
the voters in each area (using the October 1974 election results and
returns from the 1971 census). Further evidence is drawn from the
post-referendum sample survey in the series described in Chapter 3.

The size of the vote

About 26 million votes were cast at the referendum, representing 65
per cent of the listed electorate. This turnout was similar to that seen
in the average by-election and well above the normal local election
turnout of 40 or 50 per cent. It was, however, lower than the turnout
in recent general elections, which has averaged around 75 per cent.

Table 1. Turnout at general elections and at the referendum

			% of electorate voting
General elections:	June	1970	72
	Feb.	1974	79
	Oct.	1974	73
Referendum	June	1975	65

That a third of the listed electorate failed to vote does not necessarily
point to lack of interest in the EEC issue, or to a protest against the use

of a referendum. Lack of interest must have played a part, but there is no evidence of a major protest element in the abstentions. Only 1 per cent of the people interviewed in our post-referendum survey said that they had abstained on principle.

As in any election, part of the total abstention will have been due to the decay of the electoral register since its compilation in the previous October. Some of the people on the register will have died; many more will have moved away, and, even if eligible, failed to apply for a postal vote. Abstentions of this type increase as the register ages, as can be seen in Table 1. Turnout in February 1974, when the register was only four months old, was comparatively high. The two elections of June 1970 and October 1974 provide a more appropriate basis for judging the referendum turnout.

Even among people still resident at their registered address, some will have been unable to get to the polls because of a temporary absence from home, or because of illness, and so on. Experience of surveys among samples drawn from the electoral registers suggests that such factors will have accounted for 12 or 13 per cent of the electorate at the time of the referendum — about a third of the non-voters. The turnout may thus have represented close to three quarters of those available to vote.

As in any election, many people will have found it inconvenient to vote, because of their commitments, the weather, transport difficulties and so on. Others will not have bothered, because they could not decide which way to vote or because they did not expect their vote to affect the result.

An important difference between the referendum and a general election was the lack of active local party machinery to stir up the less enthusiastic and the less committed, to drive people to the polls and otherwise to encourage voting. The absence of such activity must have made a considerable contribution to the lower turnout.

Area differences in turnout

Turnout figures for the sixty-eight returning areas are shown in Table 2. The overriding impression is of uniformity. Fifty-four of the sixty-eight areas had polls within three points of the national figure — between 62 per cent and 68 per cent. Only in the island areas were extremes recorded: a turnout of 75 per cent in the Isles of Scilly, and turnouts of around 50 per cent in the three Scottish island authorities and in Northern Ireland.

Table 2. Turnout in the sixty-eight returning areas
Votes cast as a percentage of the registered electorate

United Kingdom	65				

ENGLAND	65				
Isles of Scilly	75	Kent		Nottinghamshire	
Hertfordshire		Leicestershire	67	Merseyside	
Surrey	70	Cornwall		Tyne & Wear	63
Buckinghamshire		Northamptonshire		W. Midlands	
Avon		Berkshire		Humberside	
W. Sussex	69	Hereford & Worcester		S. Yorkshire	
		Lancashire	66	Cambridgeshire	62
Gloucestershire		E. Sussex		Salop	
Dorset		Cheshire		Durham	
Devon					
Hampshire		Northumberland		Gtr. London	61
Warwickshire		Suffolk	65	Cleveland	60
Bedfordshire	68	Cumbria			
Wiltshire		N. Yorkshire			
Essex		Staffordshire			
Oxfordshire		Derbyshire			
Somerset		Gtr. Manchester	64		
Isle of Wight		Norfolk			
		Lincolnshire			
		W. Yorkshire			

WALES	67		
Gwent		W. Glamorgan	
Powys	68	S. Glamorgan	67
Dyfed		Mid-Glamorgan	
		Clwyd	66
		Gwynedd	64

SCOTLAND	61				
		Central		Fife	
		Tayside	64	Borders	63
		Lothian			
				Strathclyde	
				Dumfries &	62
				Galloway	
				Highland	59
				Grampian	57
				Western Isles	50
				Orkney	48
				Shetland	47

NORTHERN IRELAND	47

Turnout was slightly higher in Wales than in the rest of the United Kingdom, just as it had been at the October 1974 election. The above-average election turnout in Scotland was not, however, repeated at the referendum. In Northern Ireland the turnout of only 47 per cent, well below the October figure of 68 per cent, reflected the understandable lack of interest in UK national issues.

Table 3. Turnout at the referendum and at the last general election

% of electorate voting	Referendum June 1975	Election October 1974
TOTAL UK	65	73
Wales	67	77
England	65	73
Scotland	61	75
N. Ireland	47	68

The turnout figures for individual returning areas are not directly comparable with those for the general election. Although both constituency and county boundary divisions took effect in 1974, the two were not coordinated and the pattern is confused. Several constituencies now cross county boundaries and one – Richmond, Yorks. – is divided among no less than four counties.

This means that constituency returns from the election cannot easily be added to produce county-by-county results. In our analysis we have assumed that the votes cast for each candidate in a divided constituency were split between counties in the same proportions as the total electorate. For example, 21 per cent of the electorate of the constituency of Beaconsfield is in the new county of Berkshire, the remainder in Buckinghamshire. We have assumed that this same proportion, 21 per cent, of the votes cast for each of the three candidates in the constituency came from residents of Berkshire, the rest from residents of Buckinghamshire. Even if this convenient assumption of uniform turnout and voting behaviour across the constituency is wrong, it cannot materially affect our conclusions.

Among the English counties, turnout in the referendum ranged from around 60 per cent in the metropolitan counties (the conurbations), and in Durham and Cleveland, to around 70 per cent in the South-east. The variation was much the same as in the October 1974 election, the referendum turnout generally being 7 to 10 percentage points below the election turnout. The most marked exceptions were, on the one hand, Greater London and Surrey, where referendum turnout was only 4 or 5 points below the October level, and on the other, three rural counties — Cambridgeshire, Norfolk and Salop — where it was down by 12 or 13 points.

As in general elections, turnout varied with population density. In both the most densely and the most sparsely populated counties, turnout was slightly lower than elsewhere, averaging 63 per cent in the former and 65 per cent in the latter, against 67 per cent in the rest of England.

The Welsh counties showed even less variation in turnout — from 68 per cent in Gwent to 64 per cent in Gwynedd. This uniformity occurred despite some marked differences between the counties in party political and employment patterns. The variation from county to county was in fact smaller than in the October election. Then there were three counties in which Plaid Cymru and the Liberals between them polled more than a third of the vote — Dyfed, Gwynedd and Powys. This was accompanied by an above-average turnout, 80 per cent compared with 75 per cent in the rest of Wales, a pattern that was not repeated in June.

The drop in turnout in Scotland between the October election and the referendum — of 15 points — was fairly uniform across the twelve returning areas. In the three island areas turnout was about 10 points below the mainland level, but this had been the pattern in October too.

The referendum pattern was thus generally close to that seen in October. The slightly wider range of turnout figures in the referendum — from 50 per cent to 70 per cent, compared with 65 per cent to 75 per cent in the election — reflected only a lower level of interest in the EEC issue in Scotland and Northern Ireland.

Other variations in turnout

Turnout at the referendum did not vary greatly from one returning area to another. But even the small variations among the counties of England and Wales point to differences in turnout between various sub-groups of the electorate.

In particular, the numerous census measures of occupation, social class and economic well-being were all correlated with turnout at the county level. Generally, the differences were small. For example, the average turnout in the ten counties with the highest proportion of workers employed in non-manual occupations was 5 points higher than the average turnout in the ten with the lowest proportion of non-manual workers.

The absence of major variation in the published turnout figures stems largely from the counting system adopted. Greater variation is observed by considering the results of the post-referendum survey, which allow us to relate turnout to individual demographic characteristics. These results are shown in Table 4. Overall, 76 per cent of the survey respondents claimed to have voted at the referendum, against the official figure of 65 per cent. Although part of the difference could reflect some element of overclaiming, the main cause is the different basis of calculation. The official turnout figure is based on the total number of electors registered. The survey estimate relates only to those available to be interviewed. To the extent that survey non-respondents coincided with people unavailable to vote in the referendum (e.g. the sick, the movers, those away on both occasions) we must expect the survey to produce a high turnout figure. If we assume a 10 per cent overlap, a claim of 76 per cent turnout among survey respondents represents only 68 per cent of the total electorate — very close to the official estimate.

Table 4. Turnout among demographic subgroups

% claiming to have voted	Referendum June 1975	Election October 1974
All electors	76	88
Men	76	89
Women	76	86
Aged under 30	65	80
Aged 30 and over	79	90
Professional & managerial*	85	91
Other non-manual	78	86
Skilled manual	77	90
Semi- & unskilled manual	67	83

* The occupation of the head of the household

Table 4 shows that turnout was markedly lower among young people and among semi-skilled and unskilled manual workers and their families, and especially high among professional and managerial workers. But

even these differences seem to reflect general political involvement
rather than interest in the specific issue of EEC membership. A closely
similar pattern emerges from respondents' claims to have voted in the
previous October.

Moving from demographic classifications to political affiliations,
we see from the county results that turnout was lower in Labour
areas. In the fifteen counties of England and Wales where Labour
captured 45 per cent or more of the vote in October 1974, the
average turnout was 63 per cent, against 66 per cent elsewhere. But,
again, this small difference does not seem to represent a reaction to
the specific issue of EEC membership. Turnout at the October election
was also below the national average in these fifteen counties. The
explanation is that Labour support is stronger in those counties whose
residents are generally less prepared to turn out and vote.

Variations in the level of support for the nationalist parties in
Scotland and Wales had no marked effect on the referendum turnout.
In the one Scottish region in which the SNP share of the vote was less
than 20 per cent (the Borders) and in the two mainland regions where
it was more than 40 per cent (Tayside and Central), turnout was no
different from that in the rest of mainland Scotland. Similarly, the
uniform turnout in Wales occurred despite considerable variation
between counties in the Plaid Cymru share of vote – from 4 per cent
in South Glamorgan to 26 per cent in Gwynedd.

Although turnout at the referendum was lower than at recent
general elections, therefore, it followed a very similar pattern. The pro-
and anti-EEC campaigns did not overcome the reluctance of some
groups in the population to turn out and vote. But the issue neither
accentuated familiar differences nor created new ones.

The verdict

Overall, as Table 5 illustrates, 67 per cent of the votes cast were for
staying in, 33 per cent for getting out. The greatest support for continued membership came from English and Welsh voters. The Scots were
less enthusiastic, fewer than 60 per cent voting 'Yes', and Northern
Ireland returned only a bare 'Yes' majority.

The verdicts of the sixty-eight returning areas are shown in Table 6.
Only two areas returned 'No' majorities: the small island areas of
Shetland and the Western Isles. In the remaining areas the 'Yes' majority
ranged from around 55 per cent in the northern parts of Scotland and
in Northern Ireland to around 75 per cent in several counties of England
and Wales. The range of votes was even smaller within England and

Table 5. The 'Yes' majority

	'Yes' votes as a % of all votes cast
TOTAL UK	67
England	69
Wales	65
Scotland	58
N. Ireland	52

Wales, where forty-five of the fifty-four counties returned 'Yes' majorities of between 65 per cent and 75 per cent.

The uniformity of the vote must not be mistaken for unanimity. However widespread the support for Britain's continued membership of the EEC, 8½ million people voted to leave. And even the small differences between the returning areas point clearly to the sections of the population less inclined to vote 'Yes'.

As with turnout, the clearest indications of differential support for membership relate to social class. The 'Yes' vote was higher among non-manual workers and their families. But the difference was not great: the survey results show that even the least pro-European group, the semi-skilled and unskilled manual workers, produced a 60 per cent majority in favour of staying in. At county level, this shows in a rather higher 'Yes' vote in the more affluent counties. For example, an average 72 per cent 'Yes' vote was returned in the ten counties of England and Wales that have the highest proportion of workers in the professional and managerial socioeconomic grades. In the ten counties with the lowest proportions of workers in these grades the average 'Yes' vote was 66 per cent. The difference of only six percentage points is typical among the various indicators of social class and economic well-being that were investigated.

Given the line-up of forces for and against market membership before the referendum, we would expect the industrial division of a county's workforce to be associated with the result. The extent of involvement in manufacturing or mining — in which industries there were strong trade union pressures for a 'No' vote — cannot be separated from the class structure of a county. Counties with a high degree of involvement in these industries returned smaller majorities in favour of continued membership, but only to the extent that would be predicted

Table 6. The verdicts of the sixty-eight returning areas
'Yes' votes as a percentage of all votes cast

UNITED KINGDOM	67

ENGLAND	69

N. Yorkshire		Hertfordshire		W. Yorkshire	
Surrey	76	Kent		W. Midlands	65
W. Sussex		Isle of Wight		Merseyside	
Lincolnshire	75	Cheshire	70	Gtr. Manchester	
Buckinghamshire		Norfolk		Durham	64
E. Sussex		Warwickshire			
Cambridgeshire	74	Somerset		S. Yorkshire	63
Oxfordshire		Northamptonshire		Tyne & Wear	
Dorset		Bedfordshire			
Isles of Scilly		Northumberland			
Leicestershire		Derbyshire	69		
Hereford & Worcester	73	Lancashire			
Berkshire		Cornwall			
Salop		Avon			
Suffolk		Humberside	68		
Devon		Essex			
Cumbria	72	Staffordshire			
Gloucestershire		Cleveland	67		
Wiltshire		Nottinghamshire			
Hampshire	71	Greater London			

WALES	65

Powys	74	S. Glamorgan	70	Gwent	62
Gwynedd	71	Clwyd	69	W. Glamorgan	
		Dyfed	68	Mid-Glamorgan	57

SCOTLAND	58

Borders	72	Dumfries & Galloway	68	Orkney	62
				Central	60
				Lothian	
				Tayside	59
				Grampian	58
				Strathclyde	
				Fife	56
				Highland	55
				Shetland	44
				Western Isles	30

NORTHERN IRELAND	52

from socioeconomic variables. Industrialisation is simply another facet of the fundamental economic division of the country. Living in an agricultural area does, however, prove to be a distinguishing factor. In the ten counties in which the greatest proportion of the workforce (8 per cent or more) is employed in agriculture, the average 'Yes' vote was 72 per cent, four points higher than in the rest of England and Wales. The counties least involved in agriculture tend to be the highly industrialised, more densely populated and generally less well-off counties from which we would expect a lower 'Yes' vote. But the counties most involved in agriculture are not those with the 'highest' class profile. Their more favourable reaction to British membership of the EEC must be ascribed to the connection with farming rather than to the otherwise dominant factor of social class.

The age structure of a county's population seems to have had only a small effect on its vote: a half-dozen counties with rather higher than average age profiles returned a 'Yes' vote fractionally above the national average. The post-referendum survey confirms that support for membership was higher among the over-60s than among the rest of the population (75 per cent voting 'Yes' compared with the average of 67 per cent).

Turning to political affiliations, we find a clear link between party support and reaction to the EEC issue. Counties with a higher Labour vote in the October election returned lower majorities in favour of Europe.

Table 7. The referendum result against Labour vote at the October election

Labour share of county vote in October 1974	'Yes' votes as % of all votes
50% or more	62
45-49%	66
35-44%	70
Under 35%	73

Note: Scotland and N. Ireland excluded

Predictably, the reverse pattern holds for the Conservative share of the vote. At one extreme, the eleven English counties where the Conservatives polled 45 per cent or more of the votes in October returned a 74 per cent 'Yes' vote at the referendum. At the other, the nine English counties where the Conservatives polled less than 35 per cent of the votes in October returned a 66 per cent 'Yes' vote.

Clearly, Labour voters were less inclined to vote 'Yes' than were Conservative voters. The county returns indicate that those Labour voters who turned out at the referendum were more or less evenly divided for and against the EEC. This suggestion is supported by the survey finding that 55 per cent of those who claimed to have voted Labour in October said they had voted 'Yes' at the referendum. Conservative and Liberal supporters, in contrast, were predominantly in favour: about 85 per cent of Conservatives and 75 per cent of Liberals voted 'Yes'.

The survey sample included too few supporters of the two nationalist parties for reliable separate analysis. The area returns for Wales and Scotland suggest, however, that the referendum vote among nationalist supporters was much the same as among the rest of their compatriots. Thus, in Wales, both the strongest pro-Plaid Cymru county, Gwynedd, and the weakest, South Glamorgan, returned 'Yes' votes of around 70 per cent. Similarly, in Scotland, support for the SNP was as high in Dumfries and Galloway with its 68 per cent 'Yes' vote, as in Fife and the Highland region, with their 'Yes' votes of only around 55 per cent. Nevertheless, the generally lower turnout reported earlier suggests that many Scots, particularly in the north, were at least sympathetic to the SNP line on Europe.

Pro-European opinions were thus more widespread among Conservative voters and among those groups of the population from which the Conservatives draw their support. Labour voters, although undoubtedly converted in large numbers to the government line, were far less enthusiastic.

The pro-European leanings of the agricultural counties, though not widely forecast as important in the voting pattern, are easy to understand after the event. Similarly, the lack of any major effect related to support for the nationalist parties in Scotland and Wales is probably explained by their lack of involvement in UK national affairs.

The area differences discussed here, and those in turnout discussed earlier, are generally small and might be considered unimportant in statistical terms. But patterns emerge from even these small differences and it is the logic of these patterns that must be the criterion for

The Voting Pattern

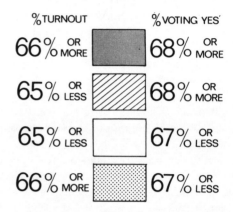

%TURNOUT		%VOTING YES'
66% OR MORE		68% OR MORE
65% OR LESS		68% OR MORE
65% OR LESS		67% OR LESS
66% OR MORE		67% OR LESS

judging significance.

The patterns can be summarised by dividing the sixty-eight returning areas into four broad groups. The division is illustrated in the map on pages 104 and 105.

First, in twenty-nine areas both the turnout and the percentage of 'Yes' votes were above average (the solid shading on the map). This group includes the whole of southern England, apart from Greater London, and extends into the Midlands and Wales. Only two northern counties, Lancashire and Cheshire, are included. Second, in fourteen areas turnout was average or below but the percentage of 'Yes' votes was still above average (striped on the map). These areas are similar to those in the first group in being less industrialised and more affluent. The lower turnout reflects the lower population density of the group, which includes the less densely populated counties of England, extending into North Wales and southern Scotland. Third, twenty-two areas returned below-average figures for both turnout and 'Yes' vote. These are the English conurbations and counties of mining and heavy industry, together with most of Scotland and the province of Northern Ireland. Lastly, three areas — the mining and heavy industry counties of South Wales — stand out from the rest of the industrial areas. They had below-average 'Yes' majorities but above-average turnout.

The overall pattern of results is simple and tidy, even to such detail as the division between commercial South Glamorgan and its industrial hinterland and the graduation through northern England into Scotland. The only deviation is that Derbyshire returned a vote slightly different from the votes of its neighbours, Staffordshire and Nottinghamshire. But the difference is marginal — a 69 per cent 'Yes' majority in Derbyshire compared with one of 67 per cent in Staffordshire and Nottinghamshire. Elsewhere, even differences of this order form part of the general pattern.

What might have been

The adoption of a county based returning system for the referendum was a political decision designed to minimise any signs of disagreement with the majority verdict. But the apparent uniformity of opinion that emerged does not seem to have been misleading. Although we can pick out groups who were less inclined to vote 'Yes', we cannot isolate groups resoundingly against continued membership.

Nevertheless, there remains the question of what the results might have looked like if the count had been by constituency. How many constituencies would have returned 'No' majorities?

In England and Wales, the characteristics of those areas less favourably inclined towards continued membership were the characteristics normally associated with a high Labour vote. The most likely prospects for an anti-market verdict would thus have been the constituencies in which Labour voters are most heavily concentrated. English constituencies such as Liverpool-Scotland Exchange, Tower Hamlets-Stepney and Poplar and Hemsworth returned their Labour members with a share of vote around 80 per cent in October 1974. Similarly large majorities occurred in some Welsh constituencies, for example, Rhondda and Abertillery. In all, fifteen constituencies produced a Labour share of the vote of 70 per cent or more.

The county returns and the survey results suggest that Labour voters as a whole produced a very small majority in favour of continued EEC membership. The most likely result even in the Labour strongholds would therefore have been a 'Yes' vote of around 55 per cent. Some MPs might have been able to persuade their own constituents to vote 'No' and some of the anti-marketeers who failed to cast a vote in the referendum might have been more willing to turn out if there had been a chance of contributing to a constituency 'No' vote.

There might, therefore, have been a few marginal 'No' majorities; nothing, however, to match the 80 per cent-plus 'Yes' votes that a few Conservative strongholds would have produced. Indeed, the most probable outcome, had the referendum count been on a constituency basis, is that every one of the 552 constituencies in England and Wales would have voted 'Yes', though in some cases only just.

The picture is less clear in Scotland. In October 1974, Conservative candidates in several constituencies polled as few as 10 per cent of the votes. But none of the other parties – not even the SNP – seems to have produced a consistent anti-market vote. The Central region, for example, had a Conservative vote of only 14 per cent in October, but still returned a 60 per cent 'Yes' vote in the referendum.

Two results for Scottish constituencies are known. The Western Isles voted 'No', and Orkney and Shetland *in combination* voted 'Yes'. Seen against the overall northward decline in support for EEC membership, the latter 'Yes' majority suggests that no other Scottish constituency would have returned a 'No' majority. The most probable outcome of a constituency count in Scotland would have been the one 'No' vote from the Western Isles instead of the two created by splitting Orkney from the Shetlands.

In Northern Ireland, the votes from all twelve constituencies were aggregated into a single return, giving no indication of individual views. The overall result was very close to 50:50 and one must assume that variation about this overall result would have produced 'No' majorities in a few constituencies. But probably none of these would have been substantial. The one predictable outcome is that there would have been some very low turnout figures.

So the carefully avoided constituency count might well have yielded only four or five 'No' majorities from the 635 constituencies — one in Scotland, the rest in Northern Ireland. Any other anti-market majorities occurring against the general trend would certainly have been very rare and very small.

Very few individual MPs would have been embarrassed by the vote of their constituents. Anti-market Labour members could have pointed at the least to a sizeable minority support for their views and possibly to a 'No' verdict among their own supporters. Anti-market Conservative members would have been seen to be at odds with the majority of their constituents, but this could not have surprised them. For the government, the demonstration of the widespread acceptance of continued membership of the EEC on its renegotiated terms would have been convincing, in some ways even more convincing than the verdict produced by the concealment of possible constituency differences.

6 THE CHANGING CONSTITUTION
Andrew Duff

The government's decision in 1975 to hold a referendum on membership of the EEC occasioned the most lively and far-reaching debate on
the constitution in many years. The discussion was pursued in books,
pamphlets and newspapers, on radio and television; academics and
politicians aired the arguments in public meetings and private
symposia.[1] The debate was finally resolved in Parliament itself.

Now that the debate and the referendum result are history, political
commentators have their chance to weigh the importance of the
constitutional innovation that the referendum represented and to
measure its effects on parliamentary and governmental institutions.
In this chapter we examine the implications of the referendum on
Parliament itself, on the traditional roles of the political parties, and on
the enlarged European Community.

A unique constitutional event?

In the discussion of these topics we can take note of experiences of
referenda in other countries. For the United Kingdom a national
referendum was a unique event, and it scarcely needs saying that
the British constitution is itself unique. In other countries the
referendum is a familiar device for decision-making, although among
the countries that use it there is no constitutional norm: in half of
them referenda are mentioned in the constitution, in half they are not.
It would be unwise to exaggerate the relevance of foreign experience
to the British case and it may be that any lessons to be learned are
technical rather than political. The government's White Paper on the
subject would tend to bear this out.[2] Nevertheless, some general points
are worth making.

Australia, Switzerland and the United States, all federations, use
referenda. So does New Zealand. In Europe, all three Scandinavian
countries, and Germany, France, Belgium, Italy and the Republic of
Ireland have used them. Among the federations, Switzerland and the
United States have made frequent use of the device. In Switzerland, at
federal level both constitutional amendments proposed by Parliament
and constitutional initiatives proposed by a minimum of 50,000
electors must be approved by popular vote — since 1935, twenty-six

initiatives have been voted on and only one accepted. Provision is also made in Switzerland for legislative referenda, which allow for most of the laws passed by the Swiss Parliament, and major treaties, to be challenged by voters.

In the United States the referendum is used widely at state level, and used even more widely at local level, but has never been used for a nationwide vote. All states use referenda in deciding whether proposed amendments or additions to the state constitution are to be accepted. Eighteen states also provide for amendments by citizen initiative, on condition that the amendment is proposed by the requisite number of electors.

Altogether, the thirteen non-federations that have used referenda have held only slightly more than thirty referenda in the last fifty years. Twenty-five have been on constitutional issues — on, among other subjects, the perpetuation of a monarchy, new electoral arrangements, membership of the EEC. Six have been on issues of community or personal life — these have included licensing hours, divorce, driving regulations.

Provision for referenda in a country's constitution is not correlated with the practice of them: Austria provides for the holding of a referendum, but has never held one; Norway makes no provision, but has. On the other hand, as Grimond and Neve point out,[3] where there is constitutional provision for changes in the constitution referenda tend also to be used occasionally for other important issues, as in Australia, where four such polls have been held.

In the British debate on the referendum, one of the arguments against introducing the system was that after one had been held there would be demands for more. Among the non-federations in which referenda have been used, only two countries, Ireland and Denmark, have made anything like a habit of them. Ireland has had six, including one on the EEC, and Norway five, including one on the same issue. Whether British referenda are to become regular or frequent events remains to be seen. What is certain is that they will be demanded on a variety of issues from now on. The barrier has been breached.

It has nearly been breached at least three times before in British history, but never before with the support of Labour politicians. In 1909, Lloyd George's budget passed through the House of Commons before being rejected by the Conservative majority in the hereditary House of Lords. A referendum was proposed and discussed but never held. Instead the Parliament Act of 1911 curbed the powers of the Lords. After that, however, the debate on referenda continued until their introduction was finally rejected by the Conference on the Reform of the Second Chamber in 1918. Several grounds were given for the rejection, in particular that the device 'could not be confined to the cases for which it was in this instance proposed'.[4]

In 1930, Baldwin stated the Conservative Party's intention of holding a referendum on the introduction of food taxes. At the time, the press was enthusiastic about the idea. Not only were Lords Beaverbrook and Rothermere behind the proposal, but *The Times* was ecstatic: 'It must be a national decision; it must therefore be taken by referendum: and, what is no less important to an impartial result, the fate of the Government of the day must not be regarded as being at stake.' Baldwin's pledge to hold a referendum was never withdrawn. But the issues changed and the question did not arise.

Finally, in 1945, Churchill proposed a referendum on whether the wartime parliament should be prolonged. Attlee's response was forthright and adamant:

'I could not consent to the introduction into our national life of a device so alien to all our traditions as a referendum, which has only too often been the instrument of Nazism and Fascism. Hitler's practices in the field of referenda and plebiscites can hardly have endeared these expedients to the British heart.'

So during this century alone, national referenda have been mooted every now and again, but in the past, as Braham and Burton point out, each time 'with a hint of drowning men clutching at straws'.[5] and each time by a Conservative or Liberal politician. Philip Goodhart, MP, summed up our national relationship with referenda by acknowledging that 'the idea of a referendum may not have been born in Great Britain, but it has certainly lived here long enough to claim naturalisation as of right'.[6]

The constitutional debate of 1974-5 was unique in that it resulted in an effective violation of the principle of parliamentary sovereignty. In 1975 an issue on which Parliament had already expressed its will and passed legislation was referred directly to the people. The government declared its intention of being bound by the referendum result even if it ran against the will of Parliament and counter to its own recommendation. There is no provision for this action in the theory of the British constitution and no precedent for it in British constitutional practice.

The referendum and Parliament

The referendum was an apt demonstration, if any were needed, that the classical position of Parliament in the constitution has been drastically modified. Parliament may still talk about what it likes and still act as it thinks fit: there has been little or no derogation in its power to please itself. But the diminution of parliamentary sovereignty by the introduction of a referendum signifies a defeat for the representative institutions to which the British have grown accustomed.

To those who adhere to the views of Edmund Burke, a member of parliament is elected to represent, at his own discretion, the interests of the nation at large. In these circumstances, clearly, Parliament has an absolute power to change the constitution. But another constitutional theory contradicts the first. If the MP is merely a delegate mandated by his constituents, he must refer to them when he is confronted by legislation on constitutional change. The first theory implies that Parliament has the final responsibility for decision, whether or not there has been consultation of the people. The second theory implies that the result of a direct reference to the people on the question in hand will be binding on Parliament.

Burke's electorate was about 4 per cent of the total population: full adult male suffrage was not achieved until 1929. As the franchise widened over the years, it became necessary for MPs to attempt to reconcile their responsibilities as legislators for the nation with their responsibilities as representatives of constituents. As Mackintosh has written, it was to 'strike this balance between expertise and public acceptability that parliamentary democracy was developed. It is this balance that will be undermined by the introduction of referenda.'[7]

Populism has not had the great part to play in British history that it has, for instance, in French, although the Labour left has always gleaned most of its support from outside Parliament and tends to regard the function of government, and therefore of MPs, as reinforcing the efforts of trades unions and working people. Generally, however, parliamentary sovereignty has been preferred in Britain because it has been able to outride periods of social conflict and give a voice to political minorities. The nation has as a result enjoyed moderately stable government, and only recently have there been serious anxieties in Britain about the role of parliamentary government. Similar anxieties about the representative capacity of existing institutions in all parts of the world have led to demands for greater citizen involvement through, for example, more devolution and greater use of referenda. But as Alderson has commented: 'The question relevant to referenda is whether the citizen can see the state's interest better than the legislator can see the citizen's.'[8] The parliamentary debates leading up to the referendum were characterised by discussion of this question, and of how a referendum could and should be used.

There are two widely differing views on referenda, one upheld by Tony Benn, MP, and others, one by Harold Wilson, MP, and others. The question of parliamentary sovereignty lies at the heart of the division. Mr Benn holds the view that referenda can answer some of the problems of representation in a democratic system that has become inflexible and unresponsive to the popular mood. Some MPs of all parties share this opinion, believing that referenda enlarge the public's role in the nation's legislative processes.[9] Many people have come to believe that the public should participate in economic and social planning at all relevant levels of government and some — though fewer — believe that workers should be involved in decision-making in individual industries and businesses.

Only a few years ago, the orthodox view among MPs was hostility to the idea of an experiment in direct democratic consultation. Most believed that Parliament could, and should, decide any issue. On several occasions the leaders of the two main parties went on record as opposing the holding of a referendum on Britain's entry to the EEC.[10] 'Parliament can judge completely as to whether it is in the interests of the country to go into the Common Market or not', said Edward Heath, MP.[11] During the election campaign in May 1970 he expanded this theme: 'I have always said that you couldn't possibly take this country into the Common Market if the majority of people were against it, but this is handled through the Parliamentary system.'[12] His faith in Parliament received support from Mr Wilson. Parliament could take the decision 'with a full sense of responsibility, with a sense that reflects national views and national trends', Mr Wilson said.[13]

During the Parliamentary session of 1971-2, several MPs (including the Liberal leader Jeremy Thorpe, MP) would have preferred a general election called by a Conservative government committed to EEC entry on negotiated terms, rather than either a referendum or a direct parliamentary decision. The Labour Shadow Cabinet's support for an amendment by the Conservative MP Neil Marten (providing for a referendum) was, perhaps unwisely, generally regarded as little more than a tactical move for party advantage. Much credit should go to persistent advocates of the referendum, such as Mr Benn, who never sought to deny that the procedure was a constitutional innovation of the highest magnitude. 'The whole of British democracy has been about *how* you take decisions', Mr Benn once wrote to his Bristol constituents, 'and this has always been seen to be more important than what the decisions were.'[14] Mr Wilson himself accepted as late as June 1974 that a referendum 'fundamentally changes the whole basis of our democracy and of parliamentary control'.[15]

In January 1975, on the day the Prime Minister announced in the House of Commons that the Government had decided to hold a referendum rather than another election, the Tribune MP Norman Atkinson wanted the Cabinet decision on the EEC delayed until after the special Party Conference. Mr Wilson replied:

'the constitution of the Party lays down that the Party was set up to secure seats in Parliament, at which we have not done too badly over the years. It was not the purpose, having done that, to say that those who had been elected to Parliament should not be able to play their full part in the parliamentary sovereignty of this country. Parliamentary sovereignty is, in fact, one of the issues in question in the Common Market negotiations. Therefore, while I have always paid the fullest attention to decisions whether of the conference or of the National Executive Committee, all of us in this House have been elected to take decisions and as long as I am Prime Minister there will be no derogation in this matter . . . The Labour Government were elected on a manifesto which pledged us to this referendum . . . We shall put this matter to the country, and as far as the Government is concerned — let there be no doubt about this — we shall accept the verdict of the people.'[16]

Despite Mr Wilson's assertions, many MPs from the Prime Minister's own party remained unconvinced. John Mackintosh, MP, one of the most articulate constitutionalists in the Commons, said that it was a sad day, 'the first historic time that a public announcement has been made that the House is fundamentally unfit to take a major decision affecting the country'.[17]

The tone of the government was almost apologetic. The majority of the Cabinet insisted that the referendum was being held on a particularly weighty issue that divided all parties, and that it was no part of the government's strategy to see a referendum used again. In the preface to the Referendum White Paper it was claimed that the Common Market was 'unique' and 'has fundamental implications for the future of this country, for the political relationships between the United Kingdom and the other Member Governments of the

Community, and for the constitutional position of Parliament'.[18] The last point is the crucial one.

In November 1974, some four months before the referendum was officially announced, the Conservative MP Tim Renton proposed a Private Member's motion on the subject of referenda[19] that provided an interesting prelude to the main debate on the Referendum White Paper[20] that took place the following March. In the latter debate four points in particular were made about sovereignty. Margaret Thatcher, MP, in her first speech as Leader of the Opposition, criticised the government's 'new doctrine' of passing the buck to the people. Mr Thorpe asked incredulously how the government could imagine that the EEC issue was important enough to have a referendum about, but not important enough to resign over. The Labour MP Paul Rose regarded it as abhorrent that while in opposition Labour should have imposed a three-line whip on the European Communities Bill of 1971-2, but that once in government it could sacrifice collective Cabinet responsibility on the renegotiations.[21] And, in support of the government, the Labour MP Roderick MacFarquhar surprised the House by quoting Asquith, who had described referenda as 'possibly the least objectionable means of untying the knot in some extreme and exceptional constitutional entanglement'.[22] At the end of the March debate, over fifty MPs abstained in a vote with a three-line whip, and the government had a comfortable majority of fifty, the size of which surprised several commentators.[23] Edward Short, MP, the minister primarily responsible for the referendum legislation, had summed up the case admirably. 'The issue continues to divide the country', he said. 'The decision to go in has not been accepted. That is the essence of the case for having a referendum.'[24]

The second reading of the Referendum Bill took place on 10 April 1975. Although the debate was punctuated by several hard-hitting speeches on the principle of referenda, by this time, it seemed, most MPs were more interested in the form that the referendum would take. Most of the eighty amendments tabled during the Committee stage of the Bill (taken, as is customary for constitutional measures, on the floor of the House) were on the form of the count and the size of the turnout in the referendum.

As a result of the pressure, the government eventually surrendered its preference for a single national count of the results in favour of counting by counties. But it did not rise to the bait offered by Michael Stewart, MP, that a predetermined percentage poll should be set, below which the result would not be valid.

The second reading thus saw the Bill accepted in principle, having suffered surprisingly few substantive attacks. One point frequently mentioned, however, raised the tantalising question of whether the referendum was as binding as the government had promised it would be. It was succinctly put by David Steel, MP, then Chief Liberal Whip: 'A referendum cannot do anything that Parliament cannot do, and Parliament could reject everything that a referendum may do.'[25] This general point was, however, roundly attacked by the Labour MP Christopher Price, who thought that the pro-marketeers wanted to undermine Parliament in an elitist way. 'I hope', he said, 'that this will be the first in a long series of referenda, so that we will be able to diffuse the aura of total sovereignty – an aura in which, in a smug and self-satisfied way, we like to bathe – and to extend democracy in many other ways'.[26] The Conservative MP Maurice Macmillan disagreed fundamentally with this view of parliamentary democracy. The referendum, he said was 'an admirable method of substituting demogogic for democratic government and as justifying the abandonment of the rule of law'.[27]

The opposition of the Conservative Party in both Houses of Parliament to Labour's referendum was, in the end, more symbolic than actual. A possible strategy for them would have been to campaign for abstention in the hope that a low referendum turnout would discredit the government. This was the plan adopted by the Socialists in France over M. Pompidou's 1972 referendum. Another tactic would have been to threaten obstruction in the House of Lords. Several Tory peers were, it seems, prepared to use their constitutional right in this way, but the dominant figure of Lord Hailsham curbed any realistic attempt at this manoeuvre. The tone in the House of Lords was set by a crossbench peer who was also a member of the European Parliament, Lord O'Hagan: 'Although, as a Parliamentarian, I regret that the mechanism of choice may well be a referendum, if the other place – the elected House of Parliament – chooses to limit its authority by setting up such a procedure, I, as a democrat, accept that.'[28] It was left to Lord Wigg, an ex-Labour minister, to inject a new reason for holding a referendum: 'It is that for three weeks the mind of the country is concentrated on great issues. Of course the public do not understand the details; they do not want to. But they can take the broad decision to come in or stay out [sic] . . . By and large, I believe in the sovereignty of Parliament. Because we were taken in as we were, when we were promised we would go in only with our full-hearted consent, I want the referendum in order that the public may be educated.'[29]

The Bill passed through the House of Lords on 6 May 1975, receiving Royal Assent on 8 May. The referendum one month later closed the issue. It was never clear what would have happened if the will of the people had contradicted the will of Parliament. The government had declared its intention of being bound by the results even if its own recommendation to the voter was thereby overturned. In the event, once the referendum was over, Parliament took no official recognition of the result.

The referendum and the parties

Some commentators have claimed that the introduction of the referendum was a direct consequence of a breakdown of the party system. Certainly, the Common Market issue was a subject of deep ideological and emotional division within rather than between parties. The anti-market case in particular promoted some strange alliances from all political parties inside Parliament and from some less orthodox appendages outside it, such as the National Front and the Communist Party. Together the allies ensured first that opposition to membership of the EEC was kept alive, and subsequently that the case for the referendum was continuously promoted.

At the same time, a bandwagon for a centrist coalition of the moderate elements from the three major parties began to move forward. Support for a government of national unity reached the height of fashion during the summer of 1974, when rapid inflation had compounded the difficulties of both Conservative and Labour parties in maintaining effective government through 'consensus politics'. The leading moderates from the major parties were, by and large, pro-market. The presence on one platform, during the referendum campaign, of Roy Jenkins, MP, Edward Heath and Jeremy Thorpe received extensive and generally favourable publicity. What lasting importance to attach to these pro- and anti-market alliances and the coalition fad may not be evident for some time. In retrospect, to take a comparable situation in France, it may be argued that the French referenda of 1969 and 1972 were catalysts to a shift in party loyalties that gave fruit only in the *majorité présidentielle* of M. Giscard d'Estaing in 1974. Like many of the predictions and hopes that were fashionable before the British referendum, talk of a new 'Euro-coalition' that would transform the face of British politics by giving form to the shifting of party allegiance has proved, at least for the moment, to have been overdramatic.

In the two Scandinavian countries in which referenda on EEC

membership were held, and in Britain, the governing socialist parties suffered the greater divisions and crises of confidence over the issue. But in Britain the practical effect of the renegotiation of terms of membership and of the referendum itself has been to resolve, if temporarily, the deep-seated and long-standing conflict within Labour over the Common Market. The coalition that is the Labour movement may have lost some credibility in the process, but it has survived.

The conversion of Mr Jenkins to the referendum idea was at least partly the result of his conversion to the belief that a cautious referendum campaign was the only means of preserving Labour's unity. In April 1972 he had resigned from the Shadow Cabinet on the very issue of the referendum. In his letter of resignation to Mr Wilson, Mr Jenkins had called the referendum 'a splendid weapon for dema-gogues and dictators'. He continued:

'This raises the wider issue of whether a referendum on this or any other subject is intended to encourage the public to express its view purely on the merits of a question *without the attempts to mobilise party loyalties* [author's italics]. I doubt if this would ever work in practice, although if it did the result would be a very substantial undermining of the existing systems of parliamentary responsibility. Governments would find it still more difficult to carry out coherent and consistent policies . . . This constant shifting of ground I cannot accept.'

Within three years Mr Jenkins had 'embraced the device with no en-thusiasm'.[30] The experiment would, he reasoned, enlarge the forum of controversy from the narrow confines of one political party to the national dimension. In the process the pressure within Labour could be dissipated. Roy Jenkins himself became President of the all-party Britain In Europe organisation, an implicit aim of which was to play down those same party loyalties that in the past he had been so anxious to preserve.

In this light, the motives of those who supported the idea of a referendum because they foresaw a consequential restructuring of party politics must seem ill-judged. Not least in this category was Enoch Powell, MP. During the passage of the European Communities Bill through Parliament he had been sceptical about the use of referenda: 'I regard a referendum as being difficult to reconcile, even on a matter of this unique character . . . with responsible parliamentary government as we have it in this country.'[31] He spared no effort to

drag the issue of the Common Market into electoral politics and it was
his failure in this regard that eventually converted him to the referendum idea. He failed because the bipartisan European policies of the
leadership of the two major parties proved remarkably resilient even at
the most hesitant moments of the Labour Government's renegotiation
of 'Tory terms'. That an electorate whose choice consisted of an
embarrassment of pro-EEC parties was thereby denied a valid democratic decision on that issue seemed to many pro- as well as anti-
marketeers incontestable. It does not follow that the rest of Mr
Powell's reasoning – that the existing party line-up was artificial and
irrelevant – was as widely accepted.

Hardly surprisingly, the diminution in the authority of the
political parties during the referendum campaign was resisted by many
party activists. The strategy of the Labour Campaign for Britain in
Europe, for example, was both to maximise active help for the 'Yes'
cause within the Labour movement and to maximise the Labour vote.
Some anti-marketeers in the party wanted to control the Transport
House, constituency and trade union machinery for their own cause.
It was only because the more zealous participants in the campaign were
less successful in the pursuit of the goal than they would have wished
that the party structure was not split. Roy Jenkins' caution was
prudent.

Many MPs from all parties did no campaigning at all. The Liberals'
activities were restricted by the financial hardship caused by two
strenuous elections in the previous year. The Tory Party machine,
and Tory loyalties, were largely submerged within the pro-market
organisation, Britain in Europe. The new Conservative leader,
Margaret Thatcher, played no major part in the campaign. The
Conservative Party in Parliament had not opposed the introduction of
the referendum energetically anyway. Labour was incapacitated because
of its divisions. At the Special Party Conference in April only 452
constituency Labour parties sent delegations. So the political parties,
per se, were less energetic and less in evidence in the referendum than
they had been in a national poll for decades.

To some extent the two umbrella organisations, Britain in Europe
and the National Referendum Campaign, assumed the role that the
parties play in election campaigns. Substantial numbers of party
politicians and workers as well as many people with no experience of
electoral politics were involved. The histories of the two bodies offer a
subject for extensive research: while the anti-market organisation has
now almost disappeared at both the national and local level, several of

the groups formed under the auspices of Britain In Europe have continued as local branches of the European Movement. In a future campaign, say, for direct elections to the European Parliament, these groups are likely to play an important part.

The greatest implications of these organisations for the political system were in relation to the government. As the Liberal leader observed during the Commons debate on the Referendum White Paper, the allocation of taxpayers' money to the two bodies, the one run by a retired diplomat, the other by an obscure lawyer, created a precedent of particular relevance to current discussions on public funding of political parties. The government had no qualms about exalting the status of the two groups. The analogy that it used was with government consultation with the broadcasting authorities at election time. During the drafting of the Referendum Bill, however, the Lord President's office paid at least as much attention to the views of the two umbrella organisations as it usually does to the traditional inter-party talks on constitutional questions.

The attempt in the run-up to the referendum to move the emphasis away from the party as the principal channel of political forces and the chief forum of debate was only one of several signs of a weakening of the role of political parties in recent years. The talk of coalition is in itself witness to a slackening of party identification. The major parties' share of the vote has fallen dramatically, and in both the elections of 1974 a majority of MPs was elected on a minority of the vote. The trend is not restricted to the two parties. The results of the referendum vote suggest that, on the European issue at least, the loyalty of the Liberal and Nationalist voters to the official party line is by no means assured. Nor is it insignificant that the referendum turnout of 65 per cent of the electorate was achieved without the usual activities of the local party machinery on polling day, or that the verdict of the people was given with more conviction than in any general election in living memory.

The referendum and the European Economic Community

The question asked in the referendum concerned the United Kingdom's membership of the European Economic Community, not the kind of Community the British people wanted. Only the Liberal Party made any attempt to present like-minded European political figures at its campaign meetings; otherwise the campaign was almost entirely an exercise in domestic politics. The amount of information about the Community that the electorate derived from the campaign was therefore limited. And it is a reasonable assumption that the public knew and cared much more about the likely consequences of British membership for Britain than for the EEC as a whole.

What *are* the likely consequences for Europe? The first is that the EEC is more robust in that the prospect of secession by any member-state, now that the British threat has gone, is remote. No matter what emotional protests are stirred by any future controversy within the EEC, practical policy for all member-states offers no easy alternative to continued integration.

As a result of its increased strength, the developing political community within Europe is certain to move increasingly towards direct elections by universal suffrage as a means of introducing democratic control in place of what is now widely considered to be bureaucratic control. The emergence of a European electorate may well offer an irresistible opportunity for the promotion of European referenda. And all the arguments over regional versus national (or international) counts will be heard again in another context. Until June 1975, Britain was a curiosity within the EEC in that the practice of direct democracy through referenda was unknown. That is no longer so.

There is a second, and more immediate consequence for the Community of the British referendum. Although all the constitutional and legal requirements of British membership had been met in 1973 — Britain had passed the European Communities Act, the Accession Treaty had been signed — Britain was in many practical ways not a full member until after the referendum. Why the original decision to go into the Community (taken over 1971-2, fully in accordance with both domestic and international law) did not work is a matter for debate. Some of the blame for this was the Community's. The larger portion, however, must be sought at home, and the particularly volatile nature of party politics over the period was a significant factor. Another factor was the refusal of the forces of opposition to accept Parliament's decision. The British trade unions, for example, declined to participate in the industrial policy-making discussions in Brussels. And without this participation the Community found it difficult to administer a social or industrial policy. The fact is that neither under British law nor under Community law could people be made to participate in the Community's political processes. The EEC is, by and large, a voluntary affair; only governments of member-states have contractual obligations.

No other country was faced with this continuing internal opposition: every other country held a referendum. France held one on enlargement of the EEC; Ireland, Denmark and Norway held referenda about joining; Switzerland held a referendum on its trade agreement with the EEC. In each case the issue was resolved decisively by a popular vote. It took Britain nearly two years after joining to put the issue to the people. When it did, the uniformity of the people's verdict was overwhelming. The result has been generally accepted, and the individuals who continue to resist are becoming increasingly isolated. The TUC and the Labour Party are taking their full part in the institutions of the Community and have recognised the opportunity for wider cooperation with their counterparts in other member-states. The referendum has made membership of the European Community virtually an entrenched clause of the British constitution.

The referendum of 1975 has severely modified British political practice. The introduction of an instrument of direct democracy into what had been almost exclusively a representative system of government means that MPs can be forced to follow a policy contrary to the one on which they were elected. Where referenda are used, at whatever level and over whatever issues, the assembly of representatives cannot any longer be a true legislature; it ceases to be the only genuine forum for power-bargaining and the exclusive channel to government. Without a strong parliament the public has no reliable protection against its own fallibility: voters are entrusted with the discretion that the British have traditionally vested in their MPs, especially on civic or social questions, on which there is usually a 'free vote', at Westminster. There can be no question of restricting the use of referenda to specified areas — for example, as Baldwin wished, to the powers of Parliament, or to the suffrage, or to devolution. The British constitution cannot limit itself in this way. It will be the victim in the future, as it has been in the past, of executive will and political circumstance.

References

1.   A review by the author of this material appears in *Political Quarterly*, Vol. 46, No. 4, October-December 1975.
2.   'Referendum on United Kingdom Membership of the European Community', HMSO, Cmnd. 5925.
3.   Jo Grimond and Brian Neve, *The Referendum*, Rex Collings, London, 1975.
4.   *The people and the constitution*, Emden (1956).
5.   Colin Braham and Jim Burton, *The Referendum Considered*, Fabian Tract 434, 1975.
6.   Philip Goodhart, MP, *Referendum*, published by Tom Stacey Ltd., 1971.

7.   *Observer*, 15 September 1974.
8.   Stanley Alderson, *Yea or Nay? Referenda in the United Kingdom*, Cassell, 1975.
9.   Stanley Alderson, *op. cit.*
10. It is important in this context to straighten the record about Mr Heath's notorious phrase 'full-hearted consent'. What he actually said was: 'It would not be in the interests of the Community that its enlargement should take place except with the full-hearted consent of the Parliaments and peoples of the new member-states.' The wisdom of this can hardly be faulted: but it was never an explicit promise to go to the electorate on the EEC issue.
11. 5 May 1970, in Paris.
12. TV interview, 27 May 1970.
13. TV interview, 28 May 1970.
14. 'Speeches' by Tony Benn, pp. 99-100, Spokesman Books, 1974.
15. Radio interview, 6 June 1974.
16. 'Hansard', 23 January 1975, col. 1755-6.
17. 'Hansard', 23 January 1975, col. 1761.
18. 'Referendum on United Kingdom Membership of the European Community', HMSO, Cmnd. 5925.
19. 'Hansard', 22 November 1974, col. 1687-1771.
20. 'Hansard', 11 March 1975, col. 291-452.
21. On the decline of collective cabinet responsibility, see 'Parliamentary Affairs', Vol. XXVIII, No. 2, Spring 1975, pp. 116-9: 'The British Constitution in 1974', by Peter Bromhead and Donald Shell.
22. 'Hansard', 29 March 1910, col. 1173.
23. The result of the vote was as follows: AYES 261, of which 12 were not Tory (7 Liberal, 3 Plaid Cymru, 1 UUUC, 1 Labour); NOES 311, of which 23 were not Labour (10 SNP, 6 Conservative, 4 UUUC, 3 Liberal).
24. Col. 292.
25. Col. 1440.
26. Col. 1447.
27. Col. 1478.
28. 'Hansard', 5 November 1974, col. 357-8.
29. Col. 357-8.
30. On Thames TV programme, *People and Politics*, 30 January 1975.
31. Article in *The Times*, 4 October 1974.

INDEX

Accession Treaty, 121
Arab states, 11
Atkinson, Norman, 114
Atlantic Alliance, 6, 8
Attlee, Clement, 111
Australia, 59, 109
Austria, 110

'balance', 85-6
balance of payments, 10, 23, 27
Baldwin, Stanley, 111
Belgium, 68, 109
Benn, Anthony, 13, 15, 83, 113-4
Bevin, Ernest, 7
Blue Streak missile, 8
Britain, 3, 37, attitudes to European
  unity, 5-7; refuses membership of
  European Coal and Steel
  Community, 7-8; decides to join
  Europe, 8-9; French resistance to
  British membership, 9; party
  opposition to, 9-10, 13-14;
  first approaches to EEC, 10-11;
  renegotiations with, 11-13, 16;
  Parliamentary opposition, 13-14;
  growth of referendum movement,
  14-16; economic situation, 29, 56;
  attitudes in 1970s, 39-40;
  referenda in, 110-17
Britain in Europe, 16, 79, 80, 86-90,
  118, 119
British Broadcasting Corporation,
  85; radio, 81; audience research,
  82, 84; television, referendum
  programmes on, 82-3; rationale
  behind referendum coverage,
  83-4
British Government, *see* Labour
  government and Conservative
  government
broadcasting time, 80-1; balance in,
  84-5
Burke, Edmund, 12

Cabinet, 77, 114
Cabinet Ministers, 16-17
Canada, 59

Centre for Mass Communications
  Research, 79-80
Chesshyre, Robert, 85
Churchill, Winston, 7, 111
Commission of the European Com-
  munities, 4
Common Agricultural Policy for the
  Third World, 79
commonwealth, 5, 6, 21, 23, 37, 39,
  40, 59, 75
Communist Party, 17, 117
Conference of the Reform of the
  Second Chamber (1918), 111
Conservative government, 8-9,
  12-13, 16, 21
Conservative Party, 10, 15, 66, 103,
  111, 116
constituencies, 92, 96, 106-8
counties, 17, 100-2
Crossman, Richard, 18
Curran, Sir Charles, 81, 83, 84
Czechoslovakia, 11

Daily Express, 22, 27, 79
Daily Herald, 22
Daily Mail, 27, 83, 84
Daily Mirror, 79
Daily Telegraph, 79
Davies, Bernard, 83
Day, Robin, 78
D'Estaing, Giscard, 117
De Gaulle, President, 5, 9, 11, 25, 27
defence, 59-60
demographic groups, 17, 23, 25, 34,
  62, 73-5
Denmark, 12, 14, 68
devolution, 38
Dublin Conference (1975), 45, 46

economic growth, 8, 21
electoral register, 94
England, 99, 106
European Coal and Steel Community,
  7
European Communities Act, 121
European Communities Bill (1971-
  72), 115, 118

125

European Economic Community, 5,
8, 11, 12, 39; early history, 6, 8;
negotiations with, 8-9, 12-13, 16;
opposition to membership with,
10-11, 13, 15, 19, 26-7, 33-5;
support for membership with, 10-
11, 19, 23, 33-5; influence of
de Gaulle in, 11, 21, 25; disunity
in, 31; importance to general
public, 49-53, surmised effect of
on economy, 54-7; benefits of
membership in, 61; public
knowledge of, 65-6; cost of
British entry, 77; support for by
political affiliation, age, area,
occupation, 100-6; effect on of
referendum, 120-22
European Education Research
Trust, 00
European Free Trade Area (EFTA), 8
European Parliament, 15

Financial Times, 79, 85
France, 5, 9, 11, 23-31, 68, 109
Frere-Smith, Christopher, 85, 90

Gaitskell, Hugh, 9, 10, 27
Gallup polls, 19, 25, 33
general elections, 1959, 8; 1966, 23;
1970, 12; 1974, 48, 78, 84,
92-3, 97
Germany, 5, 109
Goodhart, Philip, 111
'The Grand Design', 19
'The Great Debate', 77, 78, 82, 90
Guardian, 79

Hailsham, Lord, 116
Heath, Edward, 8-9, 12, 14, 28, 77
113, 117
Holland, 48
Home, Sir Alec Douglas, 10
House of Lords, 116-17

impartiality, 84-6
Independent Broadcasting
Authority, 80
industrial growth, 27
industrial unrest, 16
inflation, 16, 19, 25, 31, 33, 49, 54,
78
International Monetary Fund, 6
Ireland, 12, 14, 68, 109
Isles of Scilly, 92

Italy, 68, 109
ITV, 81-2, 83

Jenkins, Roy, 117, 118
JICTAR, 82, 83

Kennedy, John F., 9
Kitzinger, Ewe, 51

Labour government, 16-17, 27, 114
Labour National Conference (1962),
21
Labour Party, 5, 9, 10, 13, 15, 21,
47, 67, 99, 103
leaflets, referendum, 62-4
Liberal Party, 21, 47, 67, 103
Lloyd George, David, 110
London, 92
Luxembourg, 68

MacFarquhar, Robert, 115
Macmillan, Harold, 7, 9
Macmillan government, 8, 19
manifestoes, 12
Marten, Neil, 85, 113
mass media, 62-4; response to referendum, 77-9; coverage of
referendum campaign, 79-80;
provision of broadcasting time,
80-1; programmes, 81-2; rationale of referendum coverage, 82-
84; accused of imbalance in
referendum coverage, 84-6; how
influenced by campaign
organisations, 86-91
Midweek, 82

National Front, 17, 117
national opinion polls, 29
National Referendum Campaign, 16,
79, 84, 85-90, 119
nationalist parties, 103
Nationwide, 82
New Zealand, 59, 109
newspapers, 85; treatment of referendum issues, 79
North Atlantic Treaty Organisation,
6
Northern Ireland, 99, 106
Norway, 12, 69, 110

Observer, 85
oil crisis, 31
oil prices, 78-9

opinion polls and surveys, analysis of,
    19, 21, 41-5, 46-9, 50-3, 56, 62-4,
    65, 66, 67-9, 70-5; in figures, 22,
    25, 26, 28, 31, 33, 35, 37, 41, 42,
    46, 47, 48, 49, 50, 51, 52, 53, 54,
    55, 57, 58, 60, 63, 66, 68, 69, 71;
    motives for press polls, 18; 1961-
    63, 19-23; 1965-70, 23-8;
    voting patterns on possibility of
    joining EEC, 37, 45-60; on result
    of referendum, 37, 41-2; in SCPR
    1974 survey, 43; on political
    party support, 46-7, 66-7; on
    importance of EEC, 60-1; on
    referendum leaflets, 62-4; on
    information about EEC, 64-5;
    on knowledge of EEC, 68-70;
    on political knowledge, 66-7
Organisation for European Economic
    Cooperation, 6
Oxford Union debate, 82

Parliament, 13, 14, 111; debate
    referendum, 115-16; effect of
    referendum on, 122
Parliament Act (1911), 110
Parliamentary Labour Party, 13, 15
parliamentary sovereignty, 111,
    112-13
pay pause, 19, 21
Plaid Cymru, 67, 97, 99
political parties, 117-20
Pompidou, Georges, 12
Powell, Enoch, 118
prices, 21, 23, 54-5, 87
probability sampling methods, 38
productivity, 8
public knowledge, 77; about
    political parties, 66; about
    politicians, 67; of EEC, 67-8,
public opinion, 13, 16, 18;
    1961-3, 19-23; 1965-70, 23-8;
    1970-2, 28-31; 1973-5, 31-6;
    in 1960s, 45; in 1970s, 39-41, 45;
    on importance of EEC, 49-53; on
    prices, 55-6; on unemployment,
    56; on the state of the economy,
    56-7; on sovereignty, 57-9; on
    defence, 59-60; on benefits of
    EEC membership, 61; on referen-
    dum leaflets, 62-4; on referendum,
    70-5; views on EEC membership
    as long-term benefits, 75

radio coverage of referendum, 80-1
referenda, in foreign countries,
    109-10; views on, 113-14
referendum, 3, 13, 33-5, 37, 41-3;
    attitudes towards, 40;
    voting by political party in, 48;
    issues in, 53-61; public opinion
    on, 70-5; regarded as general
    election, 78, 81, 84;
    programmes on in media, 81-2;
    coverage by mass media, 83-4;
    design of, 92; voting pattern in,
    92; returning system for, 92-3;
    turnout for, 93-4; turnout
    figures analysed, 94-9; by county,
    96-7; by occupation, 97;
    by political affiliation, 99;
    results of, 99-100; possible
    result by constituency vote,
    106-8; government decides to
    hold, 114; and the political
    parties, 117-20; effect on Parlia-
    ment and EEC, 120-2
Referendum Bill, 115-17, 120
referendum campaign, 16-17, 61-5;
    general response to from mass
    media, 77-9; coverage by mass
    media, 79-84; approaches by
    organisations in, 86-7
Referendum Steering Group, 88
Renton, Timothy, 115
returning areas, 92-3
Rhodesian crisis, 23
Rose, Paul, 115

Scandinavia, 109
schizophrenia, 18
Scotland, 75, 92, 94, 96, 97, 99
Scottish National Party, 67
Second World War, 5
Selbourne, Lord, 9
Shore, Peter, 67, 85
Short, Edward, 115
Social and Community Planning
    Research (SCPR), 3, 28;
    surveys (1971, 1974, 1975),
    37-75 passim; (1975), 98
sovereignty, 13, 40, 57-9, 75
Soviet Union, 5, 8, 11
Spaak, Paul Henri, 7
Stewart, Michael, 13
Suez affair, 8
Sun, 79, 88
Sunday Times, 84

Switzerland, 109-10

Talk-In, 82
television, 64; coverage of
    referendum, 80-4; programmes,
    82
Thatcher, Margaret, 115
Thomson, George, 13
Thorpe, Jeremy, 14, 113, 115, 117
Times, The, 79, 85, 111
trade, 57
trade unions, 15-16, 49
Treaty of Rome, 8,9
TUC, 13

unemployment, 21, 56, 88
Ulster Unionists, 17
United Nations, 6
United States, 5, 8, 40, 59, 109, 110

Vietnam War, 10
voting figures, 17, 92, 93-4; in 1974
    general elections, 48

wages, 23, 55-6
Wales, 75, 94, 97, 99, 106
Weekend World, 82
West Germany, 11
Western European Union, 6
White Papers, 13, 77; 1970, 27;
    1971, 29
Wigg, Lord, 85
Wilson, Harold, 5, 10, 14, 16, 23, 33,
    77, 113, 114

Yom Kippur War, 78